MEME
LAW

How

Human Social Organisms

Create Gods, Build Cities, Form Nations!

Unleash Devils, Make Wars

and

KILL Us Dead!

Second Edition

Understand the Hidden Forces that Control Human Existence

Britt Minshall, D.Min.

PRELUDE

In (the year)

Three "sweet" twelve year-old longtime girl friends in a Wisconsin suburb go into the woods to play. One hour later, one has been stabbed by the other two 19 times and is near death. Everyone asks:

"What the hell happened?"

A young man from a good family grew up attending a small town rural church. He has been the "peace loving,' 'good" son, a member of the choir and "wouldn't hurt anyone under any circumstances." Yet, with no local jobs, he joined the Armed Forces. Fifty-four weeks later he had deliberately killed an eighty-year-old, unarmed man, his two granddaughters and their two infant sons, with no apparent reason, in Al Fallujah, Iraq. His stunned family asks:

"How could this happen?"

Between 2000 and 2009 sales and profits shrank thirty million dollars a quarter and the stock lost over 10% of its value. During this slide, the Board of a major retailer increased the CEO's compensation by 245 million dollars. Business experts ask:

"Why did this happen?"

On radio panel discussion shows, including America's renowned Diane Rehm, experts cover horrific events and invariably someone will ask:

"Why did this happen, didn't they know ...?"

1

Ukraine

In April of 2014, I attended a CSIS program, where experts compared 2014 with the 1914 run-up to WWI, noting the remarkable similarity in circumstances of today to those a hundred years-ago.

Moderator Heather Conley, Director and Senior Fellow at CSIS (Center for Strategic and International Studies), a brilliant, well-educated, experienced expert on International Affairs and extremely knowledgeable on nations and their actions, delivered the closing question.

She addressed her guest, exhibiting telling facial expressions, letting all of us know this was a question that needed answering. She said: "There is something that has plagued me for years:

> *"How come organizations and movements disappear and are gone, I mean really gone for decades, and then, mysteriously, reappear and come back to life?"*

She then stated her preamble again with the same urgency.

Everyone in the room sensed this was a question we all needed to see answered. To a person, we all slid to the front of our seats.

The expert Zbigniew Brzezinski (D: 12/2017), then answered:

> *"I haven't the slightest idea, but have wondered the same thing!"*

I was in the back row, "figuratively," jumping up and down: "I know; I have the answer" On the following pages, you'll find the formally unknown answers to all of these questions and answer your own inquiry as you watch the evening news: "That makes no sense - How the hell did this happen?" *you will no longer declare:*

The information, I am about to relate & relay to you is very difficult to grasp for many people.

WHY THE BOOK of MEME LAW?

There will be

It will be like fish reading about living in water. basic disbe-

It is obvious to every serious person: "our world is in big *life or* trouble." All across the air waves, seemingly at every turn, *ordinary* *denial* from Diane Rehm (NPR), to Radio China and the BBC - *you,* media, featuring the most knowledgeable of us, struggle *am I* *want* with troubling issues threatening us with oblivion. *to* Astonishingly, all one hears is "We have no idea why?" or *had* *them* "Why would they do such a thing?" (Direct quotes from *because* hosts on three consecutive Rehm shows)! This ignorance *you* of deep flow *my* events and the hidden forces that make them *are* *which I* (Meme Law) allows us to repeat these pernicious behaviors *barely* *call* generation after generation! *nothing on*

yourself by
aforementioned
The "they," in these questions, refer to countries, parties, *rebut* factions, religious groups and disparate interest groups. *my* Unfortunately, we continuously pose our questions in the *a* vernacular of personal behaviors, as opposed to group *very* behaviors. As long as we continue this pattern, we will *big* NEVER uncover the destructive forces ruling us and the *secret,* horror will continue.

Twenty years-ago, as I began to study for my Doctorate in Social Psychology (then called "Group Dynamics" i.e. human behavior in and of groups), I made an astounding discovery: "There are two of each of us and they are often diametrically opposed to each other." On July 2, 2017 on an NPR Program, Christopher Kimball, legendary host of America's Test Kitchen, a respected and nonpolitical laymen said it best: "The older I get, I have come to realize that individual people have NOTHING to do with governments."

In my 20 years of study I also began to realize that the world is not run directly by individual people, but by Human Social Organisms that are, in reality, collective formations of Human thought gathered as "MEME" structures. Those two different personas of each "ME," result in "ME, the person" existing, but rendered fairly mute in most things. That "other ME" (MeMe) acting as a member of a Meme, although mainly different from the "individual me," is the one that really impacts the world for good and for bad. Yet, each individual person suffers the consequences of his/her Meme behavior; while the Meme itself rarely suffers at all. It can't - it's a non-being.

✳ The best basic example of this process in action is a street gang (The Crypts and Bloods for example). Most people think of these as simple gatherings of people (individuals) and therefore as their member individuals each live out their lives, then also would the group they belong to do likewise. We traditionally believed that five units alone are the same as five units gathered - BUT, it's NOT so!

Five units alone may be individually good students, great children and loving siblings. Five units gathered as gang members (Social organism) may be an aggressive killing organism (Meme).

4

Test yourself. Every year as the holidays approach the TV buzzes with talk of the fear being felt by everyone returning to family and friends. Everyone is terrified. Their lives are about to be turned upside-down as individuals encounter the prejudices of their peers, no longer an individual, but now back to being part of a family (Meme).

Take Charlie, Ted and Harry. Their vocations are drywall installer, auto salesman and security guard, respectively. They each have a significant other, children and are casual members of the First Baptist Church (religion matters not). One thing most neighbors agree on is that they are: *"Nice guys who wouldn't hurt a soul."*

However, on a November night, in 1967, these three, angered at the way race relations were heading in the south, attended a local KKK rally. Within three weeks, they had killed a young black teen boy from their town who had dated a white girl. They were no longer the *"nice boys who wouldn't hurt anyone"* as they showed, now, as Meme members, they were "wanton killers!"

As they "Mimed-in" to the Klan, each became a different person. The talk show hosts, spoken of earlier, and academics in their quest for the truth simply ignore the fact, that: "most of the questions, for which they seek answers, do NOT involve "personal" human behavior issues. Rather, they involve customary, natural and all but preordained "Meme behavior patterns" that rule Human Social Organisms (military, states, religions and cultures).

(*) NOTE: *There are many references in the book to religious situations and church behaviors. This comes from*

5

my 28 years inside the religious world, making me privy to the clearest study of Meme behavior available. I do not cite these religions theologically or critically, but, rather as pure Memes acting in their natural environment at the behest of their members, which makes them perfect for the study of Meme behaviors.

SIDE BAR:

INTRODUCTORY BRIEFING

The GREATEST Challenge to Human Civilization in 50,000 Years:

Understand and Control HUMAN SOCIAL MEMES, the Basis of ALL Human Activity.

Powers / Principalities and the "INVISIBLE HAND"

The Great Mystery

Throughout history people have acknowledged the presence of "SOMETHING," "OUT THERE," which alters expected outcomes of intentional plans. Sometimes, this post personal force enhances our best intentions, Creating Gods, Building Cities and Forming Nations. As often as not it "exponentializes" unhealthy situations and is the force behind all human tragedy, Unleashing Devils, Making War and Killing US Dead. We have recognized that even the "Best Laid Plans of Mice and Men..." are constantly interdicted by this "Mysterious Force" and our best efforts are continually sabotaged.

In the Christian scriptures Paul labeled them "POWERS and PRINCIPALITIES." Paul correctly identified the symptoms, but could not identify the mechanics of the process, thus relegating his work to the area of religious mythology.

6

During the Medieval and Renaissance period (500 - 1400 C. E.), Jewish and Muslim scholars from the Middle East, wrote of invisible forces. They described these as "Arabian Knights" or dark angels and attempted to control the illusive creatures using prayers and sorcery.

At the dawn of the modern era, Economists and Modern Philosophers, found themselves being unable to explain these forces present in all human interactions. Adam Smith (1776) became stumped in his treatise, "The Wealth of Nations," as he attempted to lay out a modern market society. In the end, he caved, calling them: "The INVISIBLE HAND." Like the ancients, he was trying to fathom why: once a human effort was "out there" in the world, the end result was often a mystery and rarely predictable.

In today's world of "continual combat capitalism," with cradle to grave competition [Meme Law #15-p.68], in preparing our populations to "war without question," we name these invisibles forces in our foes "the Evil Empire" or "Worldwide Terrorists." In return, our adversaries title us "The Invisible Satan," as we offer each other up for slaughter [Meme Law #6-p.31]. In conjunction with the exhaustive work of E. O. Wilson, Richard Dawkins finally gave our mysterious malady a name - Human Social "**MEMES**."

The Great Discovery

Over the past twenty-years (1989+), scholars began to get a handle on these illusive forces by exposing their structure. These hidden "monsters' or occasional 'blessings" were in actuality just a nonphysical, preternatural, metaphysical phenomenon, therefore, unseen rather than a physical organism of DNA (products of multiple human minds connected not matter). They are the result multiple human connections in our thinking process. Memes were defined as the "connecting of Human BRAINS, which results from the evolving "Social Gene", functioning with other brains to carryout interconnected tasks." These minds work together, "Memed-up" (hooked up), even if separated by thousands of miles.

Today this process is being greatly enhanced by electronic communication technologies (social networks, computer networks). This connective power converts every "Me" involved - into a living part of the social organism: Me + Me or "Meme." The Human Synergy (enhanced mind energy) that results from this teaming-up of minds, creates the STRUCTURE (support skeleton) upon which EVERY Human Social Organism (company, gang, or nation, etc.) is built. We see the resulting organization or joint action, but NOT the underlying structure, the supporting Meme.

The expanding evolution in mass Meme building has created a great wave of change over the earth leading to conflict and paranoia. Today, mass worldwide communication has led to and an exhausting amount of new Meme Organisms mostly unaccountable to each other and to the human Community at large (ISIS for example). Traditional Social Organisms are in disarray suffering with role confusion and abandon creating a world in chaos.

Memes manifest as small as families and as large as nations. They operate as either "PHANTOM MEMES" (not organized), "INFORMAL MEMES" (casual, but active) or as "FORMAL MEMES" (organized, active and legal). Memes change forms, smaller to larger and vice versa, giant to tiny. However, once created, they last forever. Even if abandoned (Phantom), a Meme is able to be reenergized later (The Confederacy > Jim Crow > Tea Party / Russia > USSR > Russia / Pan American

8

Airlines or the Royal Hawaiian Nation, etc.) [Meme Law #39-p.137].

Most of us are involved in multiple Memes, as long as we are part of any social group (family - church - military - company - gang or club).

Our INDIVIDUAL entanglement in each Meme is regulated by the degree of our personal involvement in a Meme's existence: (LEAST: visitor, outsider; MORE: worker or member; MUCH MORE: officer, supporter or promoter; MOST: power wielder or ruler) [Meme Law #2-p.14]. The closer to the center (nucleus) of the organism we locate, the greater our say over the future of the Meme. BUT, and here's the glitch, "the greater also is the Meme's hold on us as individuals!" [Meme Law #37-p.128]

The reason Memes are responsible for the majority of civilization's misery is: "once individual persons enter a Meme (memes-up), to one degree or another, they surrender their personal concepts of morality to the Meme's ruling center."

Therefore, an individual who would never kill another person, will, with little thought, kill thousands while acting as a Meme member (gang member or active military). To reinforce the doing of a Meme's will, the ruling center often bestows loyal followers, who carry out their tasks, with titles, awards and acclamations. Those individuals who question the commands of the Meme are disgraced, shamed and often killed. Because, when outcomes are positive, people desire to take the credit, but when things go sour we want to blame some "other being."

A word of caution, however, we often forget how necessary and positive Memes can be [Meme Law #12-p.50]. The Cancer Centers of America, the Red Cross and Crescent, the Order of Jesuits, Bank of America and every productive enterprise in

9

history is a Meme. Without Memeing-up, we'd have no families, automobiles or TV sets. While it's true that Memes gave rise to Adolf Hitler, they also lift up a Pope Francis. Memes are neither good nor evil: they are simply "Human Social Constructs" [Meme Law #1-p.8].

UNFORTUNATELY: personal and social fear and ignorance, often masquerading as apathy, allow the ruling class to use the power of Memes to destroy civilization for their personal profit.

The Great Truth

At the Renaissance Institute, we have contributed by discovering: "ALL Human Social Cells (Memes), like ALL physical cells, operate under "an identical SET of RULES of BEHAVIOR." These, approximately, Fifty-five default settings in group interactions, we have labeled "**MEME LAW.**"

While each type of Meme operates to achieve a differing end result (military unit, labor union, political party etc.), and creates differing Human Social Organisms (Methodist Church, IBM, Federal Reserve Organization etc.), ALL Memes function under the same rules because they arise out of the remarkable similarities in the structure of ALL human brains.

Likewise, it is this structuring upon individual minds that explains the variables in Human Society, the caprice in Human activities - from EXTREME good to PERNICIOUS evil.

Every individual mind, upon which every Meme rides, is attached to the carcass of a wild animal. This primate is subject to the thoughts of its own "Id" (medulla, amygdala) and their instinctual emotions, amplified or muted by the Meme they create. These irrational thoughts are then transferred to the Meme of residence, manifesting as Love or Hate, Peace or War, Anger or Mercy, Contributor or Extractor - literally as **DESTRUCTIVE** or **PRODUCTIVE**.

10

The Great Question

"Why do ALL OF US need to understand Memes?" Because ALL news stories, from ISIS to Iran; from Baltimore's racial riots to continual warfare, are examples of Meme behaviors. Meme Laws are the reason behind your downsizing, the sellout of huge corporations creating mass layoffs and the reason a government can't pass simple, common sense laws. ALL these events depend, solely and completely on Meme Law. Conversely, healthy social actions: Prison Reform, Investor/Depositor Protections and Universal Healthcare, require understanding Meme psychologies to enact and sustain.

By understanding the Memeing process, **WE CAN CEASE** crying: "*Why did THEY do that?*" **WE SHALL SEE** the reality that makes or breaks our lives, and steals our children's future. **WE WILL BE ABLE** to slow the destruction of our planet from climate change, caused by GREEDY Memes acting to EXTRACT every resource from the Earth, while simultaneously, fabricating massive, unearned profits from selling voluminous amounts of unneeded goods! All these are examples of Meme Laws used to blindly control our civilization. Once aware, you will exclaim: "**SO THAT'S THE REASON!!!**" It's NOT inevitable, it's NOT God's will, it's NOT human evil, blind luck or an Invisible Hand - It's **Meme Law.**

So, while many of us are afraid of learning these great truths, leading us to an **Understanding of the Hidden Forces that Control Human Existence,** most rulers consider this area of knowledge their private domain. But with this knowledge in the hands of ALL people, EVERYWHERE, together, let us heal the world by understanding: **How Social Organisms work** and harness their power to create mass good instead of War and evil

END SIDEBAR

11

I//: MEMES DISCOVERED

You've never seen one, me neither. I've never touched one, you can't buy one. I, nay, WE, did not know that they even existed - although they have been the basis of civilization since we began our journey thousands of years ago.

I was first introduced to the term "Meme" by Howard Bloom, the famous author of The Lucifer Principal (NY: Atlantic Monthly Press, 1996), a book which, if you have not read it, you will have limited knowledge in understanding the basis of human existence. Howard does the finest job ever of unbraiding human society and demythologizing the good and evil of human existence.

He defines a Meme as:

"A self-replicating cluster of ideas. Thanks to a handful of biological tricks these visions become the glue that holds together civilization (*I add:*** "any social organism"), giving each culture its distinctive shape, making some intolerant of descent and others open to diversity. They (Memes) are the tools with which we unlock the forces of nature. Our visions bestow the dream of peace, but they also turn us into killers"** (Howard Bloom. NY: Atlantic Monthly Press 1995. *P 10*).

Upon discovering the existence of Memes and their massive impact on our lives, I felt like an ignorant fool, only to find that no one else ever heard of them either. Even now, at the New York Book Expo 2017, I was approached by scores of people, all ages, asking "OK! What's a Meme?" As a matter of fact, while Memes have always been the very basis of the Human saga, they were never given their modern identity and explained scientifically, until the 1980s by Richard Dawkins (some dispute this), the famous atheist. Actually, as in most cases, the knowledge of their existence has been with us for centuries, but as in many cases, clothed in other language, left undeveloped and considered religious superstition.

In the case of social Memes the phenomenon was first talked about definitively in the Christian Scriptures in the Book of Romans 8:38 and, again in Ephesians 3:10; 6:12; then in Colossians 1: 16; 2:5 and last, in Titus 3:1 as "Powers and Principalities." The New Testament Greek word for "Principality" is ἀρχή (arche), as in "arch over" or "Archbishop," meaning rule over (Authority). The Semites used the word "mu-shaw" to indicate headship collective or dominion (Principality).

"Principalities' and 'Powers" equal **"Memes."**

What the ancestors have labeled "Principalities and Powers" are the invisible collective mind structures, progressed to form as viable social organisms, with outward showing "skins" that indicate the identity of the "Human Social Organisms" (Family, club, the YMCA, the Democratic Republic of Congo, the Republican Party or Democrat Party, military unit or a church denomination).

Somehow, we have never thought to examine how they form and grow and adopt the rules by which they operate. These organizations are formed on Meme structures, which are invisible because they are the mind chords (telepathic brain interactions) that bond, form and connect in

13

relationship with other minds to form unseen, but powerful structures that fire the engines of Human Society.

The pioneering work of E. O. Wilson inaugurated this science of Human Social Evolution. Physical Evolution, long accepted is now only half the equation in Human Development, Social Evolution goes hand in hand.

Some Social Psychologists have labeled these interchanges as "Emotional Contagions" and set them in a tighter more limited frame than I see here. Daniel Goleman first addressed Memes as simply "ideas that spread from mind to mind." (Daniel Goleman. Social Intelligence, The New Science of Human Relationships. NY: Bantam Books 2006, p 15 - 18; 45)

One can witness this "network" behavior, showing up all across America, even in the twenty-first century. Today, police slaughter Black people OPENLY, with near complete immunity, even though Jim Crow and the KKK of the old south are gone. This statement irritates some who have police officer relatives. They say "their" COP relative would not do that. This may be true. Over 80% of police are levelheaded officers. Unfortunately, the way Meme Law works, all officers, after an incident, form up in "the long blue line (sub-Meme)." All meme members are required to "keep their "Yap shut" and the administration automatically attempts to discredit the victim. This group dynamic is discussed on pages (145-147)

ONE: Meme Law states: Memes are not sticklers for truth but, being creatures of the mind (Mental Models), actually favor myths, which when adopted, by one

strong Meme member, can spread like wildfire to all other members, often by force, often sparking untold madness but, also, may create enormous good.

This unquestioned developing belief pattern allows Sunni neighbors to murder Shiite friends. It allowed White Floridians to massacre Black neighbors (Rosebud massacre) and Christian villagers in Europe to commit genocide on Jewish fellow townsfolk. All this community based horror, was in spite of most locals claiming they personally had nothing against the community members they terrorized. Proving, again, that the Meme one belongs to supersedes one's own moral code.

But, this "Memeing-up process" can also energize other Memes such as the Salvation Army. These Formal Memes, developed Human Social Organisms, have constitutions, directors, and are accountable to the populace and may do remarkable good in the world.

Memes, themselves, always remain creatures of the mind who, when formed, are featureless, but have the arms, legs, mouths and cooperation of all their members. One thing that has the opportunity to muddle my thesis on "invisible mind connections," but must be acknowledged, is the fact that minds can work together (mind to mind) "telepathically" to form action and belief organizations.

Heretofore, "Telepathy" has been a taboo in the world of Social Science. Thus, we try to ignore it and explain it away. However, I have experienced it throughout my law enforcement career, as well as my twenty-eight years in the ministry. I have experimented with it, to see if it works and it does. It is powerful, universal and ubiquitous, all-be-it repudiated!

I have had a lady phone at 3 a.m. telling me her husband had just died fighting in Kosovo and another, their father had just died in Florida, eight-hundred miles away. One couple with their son, away in college, knew he was in trouble across the country. In all these cases there were no circumstances of danger or sickness that forewarned of trouble. The above mentioned boy in college had just returned to school from spring break at home and all was well. Yet all these beloved died or were in a horrible accidents and their loved ones called me for prayer, but at the hour they called they had not yet received any notice of trouble.

They simply called their "pastor" in tears (not usual behavior from these people) sensing, really "knowing" a horror had happened. We can go on for decades talking about mental telepathy to no avail. I only mention it so we might all realize just how powerful the instrument between our ears really is. Individual minds connecting to form a mental model (Meme) is just as normal as breathing. Like situations or connected minds in common interests selectively are especially open to this "Memeing-up" process (this explains work place love affairs).

One encouraging note on mental telepathy: several universities have formed "Epigenetic" avenues of research. Here they study where, among other major topics, the transferring of information from other than normally

16

accepted paths; i.e. "telepathy, can be explained genetically."

Over the past forty-years, telecommunications and social media have created an "Electronics Telepathy" of sorts. Now, rather than depend upon thought transfer, brain to brain, Memes communicate instantly with Meme members over the internet or instantly by "Twitter." Within a Nano-second, an informal Meme, made-up of 20 people in Siberia can telecast their message to 90% of the civilized world. For this reason, discussions of telepathy have become mute, and social networking has superseded the concept.

The unfortunate result of this emphasis on Internet Memes is it has resulted in the original importance and extensive nature of Human Social Memes across history and society. After all, families are not raise out of Internet contact, most companies are not formed online and almost every nation on earth predated electronic data by at least a century. Most internet Memes are informal and temporary and fleeting and of no consequence.

The work of famed New York University professor Jonathan Haidt severely attacks any connection of this telepathy theory. As he would say: we are predestined by our make up to be conditioned to accept certain positions and therefore be members of certain groups (Memes), not by encountering these mind creatures from afar off, but simply by a sort of genetic inheritance, again - Epigenetics. E. O. Wilson would ditto this aspect of Social Evolution.

In his studies, he talks of people being predisposed, for example, to "liberal versus conservative" by whether subjects prefer dots in a random pattern, as opposed to neat ordered patterns. One's choices in this theory can predict which type he/she will be. (Jonathan Haidt. The Righteous Mind; Why Good People are Divided by Politics and Religion. NY: Random House 2013.)

I believe Haidt to be 100% right on, but contradicting his hypothesis there is a "ME." I, Britt Minshall, who loves things in order and loathes disorder. Yet, I come down on the side of Liberal causes eight of ten times, even though I'd be considered VERY religious in the spiritual, moral sense (normally attached to Conservatives).

I have found this to be so in huge numbers of people who, like me, defy Haidt's logic. Yet I, like all other people, take into my psyche, from outside my realm, information that rises to emotions which should, according to Haidt's reasoning, send me running to a Tea Party rally, for example, but instead, has me on the email asking the president to stop this "awful, conservative-backed program."

In the end, even one's "choice" of conservative or liberal politics, is a non-choice, it depends almost entirely on the Meme community to which one belongs 9Faily, Friends, work setting or church). In America due to so called "White Privilege," White people are OVERWHELMINGLY conservative. The reason is simple, thanks to that privileged status, Whites have accumulated more wealth and have nurtured the most power and now wish not to rock the boat and lose the same. After all, "conservative" means CON (with or stay with) SERVATIVE (the service, from Latin *servitium*, work you are doing)

Liberal beliefs question that "privilege" and call for a change: "It's unfair, let's do it different!" Liberals (from "liberate" from the current model of doing things) believing in a more "generous" sharing of society's wealth. Therefore, they are prone to attract those that have less or wealthier people that are enlightened to the discrepancies. One of the biggest disappointments to me, as a Christian Minister, was to repeat the teachings of Jesus that model this sharing lifestyle, only to be completely rejected by congregation after congregation. They overtly chose privilege EVERY TIME.

If a person lives and works in a predominantly White world. Basic peer pressure tends to make them sympathetic to conservatives. Conversely, if one lives in a more urban, multiethnic, multiracial area and are faced with the everyday reality of inequality, they may be more pressed to stand for a change (Progressive - Liberal).

In America, a truly unusual twist has arisen. I am a perfect example. I am White, 15th generation American, a truly pedigreed "blue blood." Arriving in Philadelphia in May of 1682, in March of 1854 the Minshalls' were one of 27 families that met in Pittsburg to form the Republican Party. My family served as State Senators and Supreme Court Justices in Ohio, Indiana and Illinois (all Republicans). Congressman William E. Minshall (1955 to Dec.1974), was one of the longest serving representative from Ohio in history. In 1856, William A. Minshall, his great-great grandfather, was the first Republican elected in PA.

Yet I, being touched early-on by American racism, have stood my life, along with millions of other Whites and Blacks, on the side of Democrats attempting to secure civil freedom, educational equality and a fairer economic system to benefit ALL Americans. I am further forced to the left fighting a lifelong battle against Imperialism, militarism and wars of extraction, mainly perpetrated by my country. I have chosen to live most of my life in interracial communities and urban areas in true liberal fashion even though I do not accept the title of liberal. Rather I see myself as a Progressive - Traditionalist, kind of a Democrat - Republican like Thomas Jefferson (today called a centrist).

Now here is another "twist." Alternately, millions of White, particularly Southerners (Meme titled: Dixiecrats), feeling betrayed by the Democrats for their challenge to segregation, moved there entire Meme population over to the Republicans. As a result the Rightwing American Political Meme has become almost solidly White (I label this power force WHITE - MIGHT - RIGHT), the Left wing American Political Meme (PROGRESSIVE - LIBERAL - MULTICULTURAL) remains mainly White, but is now joined to over 75 % of Black people in the country and most Latinos, Asians and Middle Easterners.

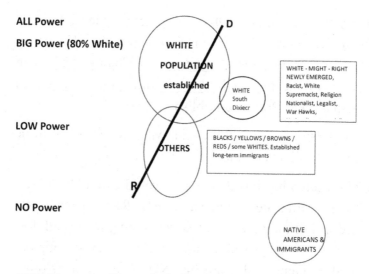

ALL Power

BIG Power (80% White)   WHITE POPULATION established   D

WHITE South Dixiecr

WHITE - MIGHT - RIGHT NEWLY EMERGED, Racist, White Supremacist, Religion Nationalist, Legalist, War Hawks,

LOW Power

OTHERS

BLACKS / YELLOWS / BROWNS / REDS / some WHITES. Established long-term immigrants

R

NO Power

NATIVE AMERICANS & IMMIGRANTS

1955 Diagram of America's Ruling Power MEMEs

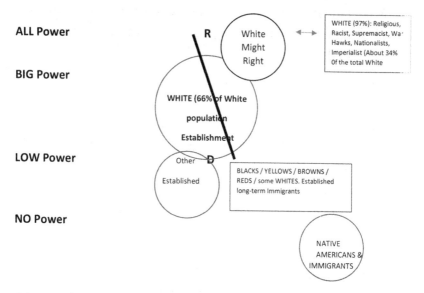

ALL Power   R   White Might Right

WHITE (97%): Religious, Racist, Supremacist, War Hawks, Nationalists, Imperialist (About 34% Of the total White

BIG Power

WHITE (66% of White population Establishment

LOW Power   Other   D

Established

BLACKS / YELLOWS / BROWNS / REDS / some WHITES. Established long-term Immigrants

NO Power

NATIVE AMERICANS & IMMIGRANTS

2017+ Diagram of America's Ruling Power MEMEs

A terrific account of the 40 development of the Right-wing Republican political power machine can be found in Nancy MacLean's new book <u>Democracy in Chains: The Deep History of the radical Right's Stealth Plan for America</u> (Pittsburg, Pa: Dorrance-Publishing, 2017).

NOTE: This is a study of social Memes and is not to be seen as a political opinion.

While I am what Jonathan Haidt would call a "WEIRD:" Western, Educated, Industrialized, Rich, Democratic (Haidt p.112), but I walk the street singing hymns all day, all while warning people not to follow most religion. Actually, many think I am just NUTS, my term (Noting Universal Thoughts and Standards). Rather, I suggest, I have simply become super-aware of the Social Mental Models (Memes) that surround us and I attempt to audit every action in an attempt to: "Live with them and not through them."

Forming Human Social Organisms, by our minds' interaction and organizing them, has been going on since the dawn of time, but we are just now beginning to define this process and identify its structure. This explains why the vast majority of speakers and teachers have not yet grasped the concept, even though it is the basis of all human social life. Social Psychologists, like Haidt, and others cited in this book, are at the forefront of finally understanding how we humans, really "super" thinking monkeys, navigate our world. Robert Heinlein, a renowned Science Fiction writer, noted, "Man is not a rational animal, but a reasoning one." (Goleman p.17)

In his now famous book, Social Intelligence, The New Science of Human Relationships (NY: Bantam Books, 2006), Daniel Goleman acts as a pioneer in the area we are examining. He calls this interaction between brains: "The Sociable Brain" and labels the study, just now coming of age, of brain actions outside the cranium, as "Social Neuroscience." He only refers to the new word, at the time, "Memes," once (Goleman p. 46), saying: "Memes may one day be understood as mirror neurons at work" (outside the cranium).

Just keep in mind that there is such a thing as minds gathered, which means there must be a human ability to form Mind Formations (Common Minds or Collective Minds). But, because it cannot be quantified, boxed and traded it is usually ignored. Unfortunately, this continued ignorance, i.e. not understanding these Memes, is the curse of Human Society and the cause of continual repetition of even the most destructive acts (Wars, Financial Crashes, and Criminal Behaviors). We, who face the future, thanks to technology, are destined to find ourselves near drowning in Meme activity and ignorance of Meme Law will leave us as victims.

II//: MEME BASICS

Memes are human minds connected, much like computers can be attached in series to form a server, supercomputer or to form a network.

TWO: Meme Law states: The social role of a Meme is to allow the Human mind to organize society by creating and operating Human Social Organisms, where LEADERS can direct; ENFORCERS can order; the LESSER connected can function and the MARGINALS can be inspired to produce.

Later, I shall refer to these categories as Alpha (Administrators), Beta (Bullies), Gamma (Geeks), and Delta (Dunces) for simplicity.

Remembering that humans created computers, it can be easily seen that all human societies are simply a series of Memes ordered like a computer, really vice versa. Regardless of which came first, like "the chicken or the egg," the omelet has to do with both. But, never forget, that while computers have helped greatly in Meme creation they are only a communications tool used in Meme establishment.

But let's start at the bottom and climb the Meme ladder to get a complete understanding of what Memes are and how they are formed. Let's go back to the individual human mind in its infancy. From birth, the mind starts to take in, process and act out on information received as voluminous amounts of data.

The brain begins to attach bits and pieces of experience and knowledge to other bits, forming what psychologists call "Mental Models" (Laurence Gonzales, <u>Everyday Survival, Why Smart People Do Stupid Things</u>." NY: W.W. Norton, 2008; pp 19-23).

Throughout our lives, we process and store information in two differing Mental Model addresses or "boxes." (1): **"Belief Boxes"** are tied to our emotional needs. Here ideas, feelings and hopes are handled; and (2): as **"Behavior Boxes"** where dexterity, abilities to act, knowledge of how to work "IT" and needed skills are processed. While working separately, the better these two work in tandem, the more balanced and usually more content a person will be. Those who have the ability to bridge conflicts between these areas are usually the most effective in directing society.

For infants and toddlers some of these fledgling Memes form as "Belief Boxes" (information gathered anecdotally to cognitively explain this new world): "This woman, who strokes me and feeds me, must 'love' me." With that, the infant begins to develop the love "Belief Box" as the mother's milk encourages a "satisfaction and safety" Mental Model based on the meeting of nutritional needs.

Conversely, if this woman does not feed me, a "distrust" Mental Model Belief Box is generated. These formations will impact the child's behavior all its life.

The baby feels hunger and desires to kill the hunger pain, so: (1) it cries, and if no food comes, (2) it cries again, and on and on until a nipple appears from its mother. (3) The child sucks and a fluid gushes into its mouth resulting in (4) pleasure and comfort. Soon, these occurrences are grouped and, the next thing you know, the infant doesn't have to feel hunger, but, at a certain time of day, it just cries and the series plays out.

As the years progress, this feeding action is added onto and if all goes well a Behavior Box - Mental Model is well established. Now, when the child desires to eat he/she opens this Mental Model, now automatically activated, and, without so much as a thought, goes through certain actions (toasting pop tarts, pouring milk etc.) and the child is out the door heading for school. At the same time the child's Belief Box structure is replenished with thoughts of safety, well-being and trust, and the child has reinforced those beliefs with action.

It must be noted here, the 25-year-old male constantly in prison, is a High School dropout who has become an angry and dangerous man, who was the child who cried and did not get the milk. These children go on to empty kitchens and empty houses. If no safety Belief Box is developed, a no trusting Behavior Box is opened and you get a career criminal. In this case, the body gets its needs met without the aid of trusted others, therefore the subject learns self-satisfaction with no regard for society.

As time progresses, the growing human repeats the pattern of first grouping actions together in Mental Models, then attaching these together, so that the mind does not need to "think out" every action. These are now attached to a person's Belief Box involving his/her concept of the world.

26

The person then activates Behavior Boxes to carry out needed actions, near spontaneously.

At the end of life, these connections often begin to unravel, requiring the elder person to think through these formally automated tasks and, thereby, they seem to become "befuddled." Often attributed to Alzheimer's disease, in many cases this is simply dementia as the mind loses its connectedness and unravels.

Now, back to the child. Without these Mental Model - Behavior Boxes this would be his/her typical morning Program Schedule:

1. Arise (scratch head, look out window, face disgust, disrobe, check mirror image)

2. Wash (turn on water, get soap, scrub)

3. Urinate (discard underwear, engage toilet, etc.)

4. Brush teeth (get brush, measure paste, add water)

5. Replace brush

6. Evacuate (at least sit on the toilet and pretend)

7. Dress (first underwear, right sock, left sock, shirt, pants)

8. Put on Shoes

9. Go to the kitchen

10. Signal Mom for food needs

11. Take cereal from shelf - do not replace

12. Get milk from fridge - do not replace - gulp down

13. Race to door

14. Board school bus

Even this list is abbreviated. Imagine thinking through all these steps; what a cumbersome process at 7 a.m. The household couldn't stand the drama. So, Behavior Boxes save the day. The child learns to open the Behavior Box, without a word, and acts through its steps, just like a computer loads and performs by downloading the files it needs.

Now the morning looks like this:

1. OPEN: The "Start the Day" Behavior Box

2. CLOSE: That Behavior Box-done/next open Behavior Box "School."

To the chagrin of parents, the meme-up thing (working in Mental Models instead of the items list mode) does nothing for putting the milk and stuff back in the fridge. As a matter of fact, it makes it worse. Once the child closes the Breakfast Mental Model, any unfinished tasks (trash out, fridge closed, yesterday's outfit in basket) are gone, out of mind, out of sight - GONE.

To illustrate the power of boxing gone bad is found in the tragic outcomes, as recently reported on TV (many times each year), when a loving father put his two year-old child in a rear safety seat and drove to work, forgetting to drop the child at the daycare. He locked his truck with the child inside and she suffocated. This happens over thirty times a year and most of us become furious at the parent. In reality, in most cases, the parent was only guilty of automatically closing one Mental Model (Family) and opening another (Work) and no longer had knowledge the child was there. So, consequently: it's a dead child; a ruined marriage and often a long undeserved prison term. Armed with this basic of Meme Law, your help tip is: DO NOT use rear seat safety seats, or if you must, put a red window sticker on the driver's side window with BIG yellow letters "CHILD!"

But now you see how powerful and life changing a force Mental Modeling is. It's how and why the human brain naturally develops the Meme making process, which is in effect journeying through life, using a series of these Mental Models (boxes), grouping life's activities with beliefs. It is the growing child's training and acceptance of this embryonic "Memeing-up process," (creating Behavior and Belief Boxes) that will decide where he/she fits into society.

A person not good at boxing beliefs and action will have a tough time living as an individual, but have a worse experience forming a family or growing educationally through institutional learning. This is why children missing a solid family experience are at such a disadvantage, they have little experience forming their Belief Boxes and using Behavior Boxes. With no experience at family dynamics they lack trust, order and safety - the very FIRST precept of the Memeing process.

We'll speak of it later, but persons with extreme difficulty "Memeing-up" or "in" with others, who are better developed in this area, often find themselves a lower level career or become career military people. Here, they adopt

29

the basic Behavior Box of organized military life or a
disciplined thought free dynamic and let it become their
social platform. It should be noted that in the United States,
prisons offer the same opportunities. Some
underdeveloped social personalities (remember the child
going to school unfed and uncared for and angry) become
attached to prison life and actually reoffend to get off the
streets into the safety of the prison Meme (like a family
organism). See DIAGRAM #1, below:

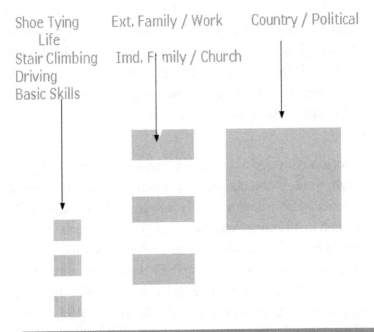

Shoe Tying Ext. Family / Work Country / Political
Life
Stair Climbing Imd. Family / Church
Driving
Basic Skills

We Think In Modules (Belief Boxes/Mental M.=Memes)

So, now, one can see how Memes are a basic function of
the brain. It becomes easy to extrapolate. Just as we box
our own life's personal functions, we also "box-up"

(meme-up) the world around us. Just as we do not double think the contents of our personal Belief and Behavior Boxes, we do not second guess our lives as part of a Meme. The next time you need to tie your "tie-tie," think it through. You can't do it; you've forgotten how to tie it by repeatedly doing it in a Behavior Box.

The next time you ascend stairs, don't try this while descending, you're liable to fall flat on your bum, think through each step. When not thinking you can do it easily, but, if you "try" to do it, you stumble.

In both cases, you were thinking outside the box. From birth, our minds accept mental modeling (boxing): first personally, next, with family, in school and in vocation. Our entire life is Meme living. Forming civilizations is doing the same thing but with thousands of other people.

Our politics and religions become sub-dominate to the cultural and national Memes to which they belong. This "God and Country" packaging actually supplants any "think through process" an individual would normally ascribe to such high and lofty beliefs. This group has made war and state sponsored violence a regular way of life.

Tribal warring, an ancient and continuing plague upon humanity, works under the same principle. If you are reared in a Hutu family in Rwanda surrounded by anti-Tutsi religion, stories and education that teach "Tutsi's are human scum," even if you swear to yourself, that you are not prejudiced, without strong personal mind intervention, you will kill on demand.

31

III//: MEME GATHERING

If you ever want to see what it looks like as a Meme gathers, go to a university science lab. Watch as lab workers make-up slides with bacterial cultures on the glass. As the minutes go by, look into the microscope and watch the culture multiply over the slide. They grow, connect and multiply. This is like Meme structures, except in the physical instead of the mental realm.

Now, in the case of the bacteria, each strain recognizes other like bacteria by chemical and biological markers allowing biofilm to form. So, also, imagine minds passing in the night. While independent of each other (like say the bacteria on the starting slide are solos) their minds' thoughts and experiences look for markers to recognize in the others. Humans use race, language, facial features, smells or beliefs to draw and bind us together. If everyone present at an initial Meme gathering is a first timer in a particular setting, they are equal, so they "meme-up." This is how a new Meme is formed from scratch.

If an individual arrives in a setting where others are already established (remember this is the mental realm, not the physical, so we're not necessarily talking of a physical location, but, rather, a Belief Box, or, if an action is needed, a Behavior Box) then one looks for familiar markers and, when discovered, the newcomer "memes-in. This gathering together process is defined as "aggregating" or massing together. (Often a Meme has become closed, so as not to welcome new members and, in such a case, the newcomer is "Memed-out").

In all cases, if the new comer does not match the marker test the meme members have set for themselves, then a "meme-out" will occur at once. The most apparent "meme-out" to recognize readily, involves the snob factor. Sororities, churches and fraternities are perfect examples. The markers used to identify a prospective Meme member are class placement, race, culture, sexual orientation, legacy and net worth. Each such group organizes themselves around "exclusivity" not "inclusivity."

I've come across churches that lock their doors, allowing only their same kind of people in. Back during Jimmy Carter's run for president, it came out that almost no Southern Baptist Churches would admit Black people. Both Mr. Carter and I left the Southern Baptist denomination at that time for that reason.

Interestingly, during the same time period, my family (White) and I, traveling on a Sunday morning, stopped to worship at a Black Baptist Church in Worthington, North Carolina. After being seated, the deacons came and escorted me, alone, to the back room, to be questioned by the pastor, who was upset that a "White man would come to my church." It took the entire hour for the congregation to accept us; no "White" person had ever visited their church in its 125 year existence. Talk about Memes being isolated from each other: the "Raleigh Observer" wrote, way back in 1980: "Sunday morning is America's most segregated hour." Which all leads us to a major tenet of Meme Law:

THREE: Meme Law states: Like kinds of Memes repel and isolate from each other, similar to like poles of a magnetic force. Unlike Memes may more easily amalgamate, cluster or cooperate.

Actually, the late M. Scott Peck talks of the fragility of Memes, although he speaks of "Community." The word "Meme" and the realization that these ubiquitous organisms work under such stringent rules, had not yet occurred to us. In his book The Different Drum (NY: Simon and Shuster, 1987, *pp 130-147*), he notes communities are held together, barely surviving internal, often competing forces - for example, "Inclusivity and Exclusivity."

Peck talks of group "tension" surrounding: "Size, Structure, Authority, Inclusivity, Intensity, Commitment, Individuality, Task, and Ritual." Although Scott writes primarily to religious and academic communities, all Memes operate under the same structural rules and experience the same tensions.

When I inaugurated the concept of "Church for Everybody," I began a thirteen-year struggle with all kinds of interests warning me that I was upsetting the religious world's "rules" (Meme Laws). I received threats from Whites, Blacks, Muslims and even a Rabbi or two. But, the most persistent rebuke came from my fellow denominational protestant pastors, who considered me a "show off." All these clergy believed churches should be "mono-cultured" and that "mixing" caused too much trouble. This "closed Meme" culture makes religion the perfect partner to any political Meme seeking to start a War. All the Ruler needs to do is enlist the priest, who will then demonize the "other religion." Then the followers will kill as ordered.

The reason is, most religious professionals, regardless of church organization, operate on a sea of distrust of other religions, which is due to endemic, visceral mistrust and fear." Religions, then promote isolation of their group from all others. This was brought fresh to mind, when the Sunnis of Iraq rebelled against the newly U.S. placed Shiite government (2014). The Sunni clerics were screaming from their pulpits "to arms, kill the infidels." Shiite pulpits responded in like kind, both of which rang true to the same situation in Northern Ireland, just twenty years-ago - Protestant verses Catholic clerics.

This reminded me of Maya Angelou's famous poem: "A Brave and Startling Truth:"

When the Rapacious storming of the churches,
The screaming racket in the temples have ceased,
When religious ritual is not performed by the incense of
burning flesh... then the world will find peace.

"(Celebrations. NY: Random House 2006, pp 18-19)

I wondered: "Where had all the clergy in these combatant faiths been, when their bunch was on top abusing some other religion? I imagine in the same place American religious are today as our Meme's (USA) interests, are setting the world on fire for our benefit - HIDING!

35

SIDEBAR:

Humans a perpetually dogged by religious wars. My hope is every reader, especially those tied "tightly" to a particular faith, will put aside ANY notion that one religion is the "ONE!" That their religion is the one true faith delivered by God -"it isn't so gang!"

Religion, ALL religions, are simply Human Social Organisms (MEMES) each attached to a particular cultural, race or geographic area, And are unconnected to God in any way. MY PERSONAL faith is very Christian - Full Gospel and I feel as close to God as any person on earth. BUT, I stand back from the "organized" Meme of denomination remembering that the Christian faith has killed, butchered and destroyed more people than any other. Everything Islam is doing currently Christians invented first.

END SIDEBAR

Today we are again plagued by wars of religion. It is easy to see why Richard Dawkins and millions of others claim to be Atheists.

And the root cause are people that believe their religion is more "Godly" than another and that somehow "The Creator" has chosen one religion over others.

My most persistent adversary in the fight to end war, injustice, hatred and disregard for a person's life and property has been Churches and religions. This has led me to the conclusion that THEY are godless and the enemy of well-intentioned people everywhere. RELIGION is GODLESS and again, it is of no connection to our Creator.

In the end it's just Meme Law:

FOUR: Meme Law states: Every Meme seeks to identify itself differently than others, seeing each separate identity as an establishing principle, justifying each Meme's own existence and rendering it superior to others.

About ten years ago, a new convert to Christianity, in an evangelical church, called me on the phone. He just "knew" a pastor of a big stone denominational church could not be a "true Christian," so he set out to convert me.

After his initial invoking marker, "Praise the Lord," and telling me he "loved" me, I never met him, but a "love" greeting is deemed necessary among Christians, especially if one intends to do you harm. Among Muslims the greeting "Praise be to Allah" serves the same purpose, as does "Hare Krishna" among the Hindus. He then set out to prove I was damned:

Convert: "Brother, do you believe in Jesus Christ as your Lord and Savior?"

Me: "Absolutely, I met Jesus March 11, 1975...."

Convert: "Well, have you received the Holy Spirit?"

Me: "Oh yes, the greatest gift of all, I've been sanctified and baptized in the Holy Ghost for fifteen years."

Convert: "But, do you have the joy of serving Jesus Christ?"

37

ME: "Oh yes, my brother, completely and absolutely everything I do is for Jesus, I just pray I get it right."

Convert: "But....I ......Mean" (hangs up).

What you read, in this very primitive encounter, was a Meme member (new convert), who had been accepted into a Church (Social Organism) as an outsider, but, who is now Memed-in. Experiencing the inclusion of "being in," he needed to talk to outsiders for his Meme and capture them, not unlike a pet cat who brings home a dead mouse. He saw me as a member of another Meme, he presumed to be inferior, less Godly than his. In other words, the only authentic marker was "his Meme's marker." New Jehovah's Witnesses are required to find converts to ensure their meme-in; that's why the door to door desperation.

In this, you see why a religious Meme should NEVER, MUST never, be allowed to play in the political world. Religious memes will never accept another religious Meme as equal. Therefore, when one ascends to political power, seen as law and authority for "everyone," in a secular society, many citizens would be excluded.

Most notably, in American Christianity, Pat Robertson's Dominionist movement sees an America ruled, not by a Senate and House under a constitution, but by a council of elders using Judeo-Christian traditions as its law (Like ISIS and Sharia Law-Same concept, different gods).

For the hope of a unified future world "under secular universal law" both Christian rule and political Islam are equally objectionable. In either case, if a religion Belief

Based Meme controls a society, all other like kinds of Memes (religions) suffer badly. It must always be so - it's Meme Law:

FIVE: Meme Law states: Individual persons have a default setting of Communion, when encountering other individuals; Memes have a default setting of Combat, when encountering other like memes. *

(*) The basis of the "default setting" concept is from Laurence Gonzales, <u>Everyday Survival; Why Smart People Do Stupid Things</u>. New York: W.W. Norton 2008.

Here's the great irony: Individuals by nature seeking "communion" need to "couple up," join in, cooperate with and partner with others to achieve anything. This "individual" partnering results in a Memeing-in or up, which in turn creates new Memes who then begin "Combat" with their fellow like Memes. The point is: "You can't run far enough to escape Human Memes." My hope for society is to understand how and why Meme behaviors are so powerful and ubiquitous, rendering them more controllable.

The main reason people flock to a "new" social entity (church or gym or social club) is memeing-up at a startup is less frightening and less risky than trying to "meme-in" to an established organism.

Another characteristic of a gathering Meme is to identify an "OTHER" Meme as an enemy of your Meme. This makes new joiners more compatible and more willing to swear loyalty.

So, upon meme-up and naming the organism, the first thing Memes do, naturally, seemingly without intent, is to identify or generate an enemy Meme (another like social organism) as a threat.

When the USSR was founded in 1917, it founded the Comintern (An external organization) to engage the world for communism and rid the world of "evil" capitalism.

Naturally, that caused an equal and opposite reaction, as the Capitalists of the west counter-demonized the USSR. The Soviets also appointed Commissars to identify the enemy within the state (Internal Dissidents).

In the fledgling USA, it was Native Americans ("Injuns, red skins"), our Meme-self pushed to get rid of "them." In Nazi Germany, it was the Jews who were victimized. Likewise, for the migrating Jews in Israel, it has been the Palestinians and, of course, vice versa, all because of this natural fear of others' Memes (outsiders).

Interestingly, during the week of October 20, 2014, a high level Israeli official remarked, on an NPR news interview, that "The Jews of Israel should be able to live anywhere on the West Bank they wanted." HOWEVER, when the NPR commentator asked if the Palestinians should be able to live anywhere, even returning to their ancestral homes in Israel proper, the official replied: "ABSOLUTELY NOT."

He explained that would "dilute the solidarity of the Jewish population." He spoke these sentiments unabashedly, with no sense of guilt. After all, HIS personal conscience was now in the hands of his Meme (Israel), which saw the

Palestinians as outsider enemies! You will recall that as soon as the White European power Meme took over the American continent, it was OFF to the reservation for Native Americans. Jews / Palestinians; Europeans / Native Americans; Spanish / Mesoamericans; Sunnis / Shiites - it's all just Meme Law:

SIX: Meme Law states: The fastest, surest way to provide a Meme with identity and member loyalty is to identify an enemy threat, either internal or external, to focus member's fears and hatreds upon.

Since WWII, power seekers (American Empire builders) in the US Government, knowing that a nation is most profitable and powerful - if it has an enemy, have acted through the Clandestine Services of the CIA (also using other government agencies to cloak its schemes), repeatedly, to set before the American people a threat we could fear.

This is not the invention of American rulers but a longstanding practice of nations since civilization began.

In recent history (1950-1990) we created a series of "enemies:" Costa Rica, Argentina, Iran, Korea, Vietnam, Indonesia, Chile and, of course, everywhere we flushed out communism, even if it was not there. (Tim Weiner. Legacy of Ashes, the History of the CIA. NY: Doubleday, 2007 *pp 1-19*). We'll cover this IMPORTANT chapter in American history later.

Beginning in 1990, seeing how successful our perceived threat program had been, and with communism on the wane, another play on "enemy" was introduced. Our rulers took the idea from Johnson's war on poverty, a good use for "war on" and carried it to a "war on drugs" and an un-named war on immigration, both external and internal threats combined. Indeed, Memes are the easiest to enliven if a threat is presumed.

The established meme in control of the U.S. has traditionally been White and well established, while both of these new "enemies" were mainly Blacks and Latino's (War on crime etc.).

You will note, there was never a "war on" WAR (except from a few stalwarts like me and Martin Luther King, who got killed, not for his civil rights work, but for his newly expressed opposition to war). There was never a "war on" excessive profits, both of which are the REAL threats to all Americans, except the power gluttons who profit from both.

As Memes gather and grow, usually early on, the earlier founders make a decision as to whether the Meme will be major and open or minor (mini even) and closed. If the reason for gathering is social and protective, that is gatherers seek safety (most churches, clubs, fellowships, support groups), a closed model will be adopted. In the Meme Dynamics chapter, we will discover how being an Informal Meme, as opposed to a Formal Meme, may impact this greatly. Members will welcome newcomers, only as long as they are nonthreatening and match the marker test. But once the organism's needs are met, even acceptable newcomers are discouraged.

If, on the other hand, the reason for the gathering is to change the world or tackle a major problem impacting many people, an open model is adopted. Truth is, even in this "open model," many in leadership continually attempt to limit outsiders joining, thinking it is harder to control the body, the more open and sizable it is.

It needs to be said that, just because the reason for a Meme's formation is open and modeled to achieve its purpose, does not mean the gathering Meme will grow. Many times the instigator of the process has grandiose plans, but, those who attach (meme-in) are coming seeking the security of the organism. In this case, the constitution will sound lofty, but the end result, will be much more limited.

An example is the World Tabernacle of God's People International, a storefront church in Baltimore, with twenty members and one part-time pastor. No matter what the pastor desires, it will never grow. She/he has big dreams and a small budget; but both the church's name and the Pastor's dream clashed with the members' desire which is a safe place to feel wanted.

An international trading company in Chicago is a similar Meme model. In spite of the grandiose name, the chances it will ever morph into its name are nearly nil. A single ambitious proprietor, working twenty-hours a day, has managed to raise a gross of $211,000 using one old truck; that's great, but usually that's it.

There is nothing inherently wrong with either small Memes or large Memes. The thing is, many people deceive themselves and those around them, envisioning an outreach to millions or promise of changing the world for the better, but are continually frustrated, not realizing their Meme model won't ever let them succeed (perhaps this is your author's fate). Memes can only grow to the capacity of the rulers' imaginations and numbers and attitudes of the minds making up the organism, coupled with their willingness and dedication to help the Meme fly.

Likewise, when dealing with small Memes (families, small retail or family business) it's not only the vision of the Matriarch and Patriarch (usually husband and wife), but their willingness to surrender all to the Meme.

Once I had a family disintegrate into divorce after 20 years of marriage. I learned in counselling that the couple loved each other, but they had given up on their Meme creation, i.e. the marriage was bad, not their personal relationship.

SEVEN: Meme Law states: A personal relationship, no matter how well grounded, does not necessarily make a good lasting Meme relationship.

Once divorced, this couple became the best of friends, doing all the best things a marriage is supposed to encourage.

EIGHT: Meme Law states: The destiny of an organism's size, structure and success is a combination of the founders' vision or the long term successor leader's vision adopted in one degree or another by the followers (cadre), which then becomes much like an organizational DNA, difficult to supplant even when the originators are all gone.

In the case of an open, major-minded Formal Meme, the adjustment comes from the founders being replaced, after the social organism is a fully formed "Formal Meme." Rarely will the add-ons (meme-ins) tolerate the presence of the founding members, especially if newcomers see the potential of the organism and they picture themselves in the wheel house.

Usually, the founders, even if beloved and well known, are perceived as short sighted and/or incompetent. Often, the added generation will wait for the founders to die off then change everything, but not always. Recently (2013) the iconic founder of the Men's Warehouse, George Zimmer, you know: "You'll love what you see," was fired by his board. Most likely the younger board members teamed up with greedy investor types to bounce the "old" and his loyal followers out. George can take heart, however. The day after he dies, there will be a six foot statue of him, and a memory wall, constructed at Company headquarters, renamed: "George Zimmer Plaza." Religions kill their prophets, then they are voted to sainthood with a statue.

Pastors experience this all the time. I was warned by an elder pastor years ago: "stay twelve years, if you can, but never thirteen; the "youngins" will want their own generation and they'll do anything to get rid of you!"

The thing to remember is: in the end, the Social Organism's leadership is completely subject to the mass members' desire. When Tipp O'Neal (Speaker of the House) said that "all politics is local" he said that every leader, no matter how highly placed, in the end, will crumble if even a small number of grass rooters pull away. Emperors, Popes and Presidents forget this BASIC piece of Meme Law.

Eric Cantor of Virginia, one of America's most respected and well supported political leaders, considered a "shoe-in" in the 2014 primary in southern Virginia, was brought down, by perhaps, 3% of his electorate.

NINE: Meme Law states: Memes, even international organizations, are always the most vulnerable at their base. Meme leaders should never forget in a Meme: Power comes from the center, but power's authority comes from its mass membership.

IV//: MEME STRUCTURING

Before any Meme is formed, it is important to remember, we begin with the Individual and that individuals seek communion with other individuals. When found, this communion results in connections from which Memes spring. From this initiating universal spring board, all Memes are formed in stages of maturation, each offering a differing Meme structure.

The three stages of meme formation are: **Phantom / Informal / Formal**.

Budding relationships, between one person and another are not Memes. (Number ONE/each circle = a person)

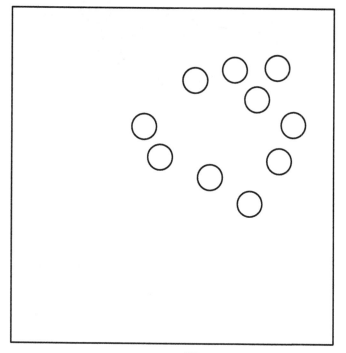

However, even in personal relationships, many of the Meme Laws apply. The selfishness, aggressiveness and needy behaviors of individual people, impact small encounters, just as these same traits form the basis of Meme Law.

Once a common purpose is found, a Phantom Meme may be created, as other people are attracted. Phantom Memes have no social organism or commonly agreed markers;

(ILLUSTRATION TWO)

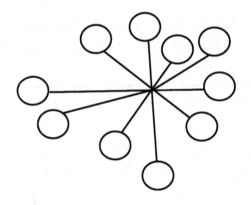

they're just a small group gathered with similar interests and, usually, similar backgrounds, say a bunch of old Greek Americans hanging out on a corner in Greek Town in Baltimore.

If a common path is discovered, like a threat or common interest, the group all recognizes, they, will usually, then come together in an Informal Meme. Say a group of men from outside Greek Town gather on the same corner. The Elder Greeks now prepare to standup to these intruders. So

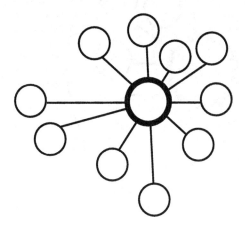

(ILLUSTRATION THREE)

they form an informal gang called "The Old Greek Men."

If, however, the stimulus continues, and is considered more serious, then they become a Formal Meme, choosing a name, picking a leader and setting rules, registering as a 501 (c) 3 as a Social Organism. The Old Greeks may rent a store front, get an occupancy permit and become The Old Greek Social Club.

In the meantime, if the outsiders intend on staying, they, too, make jackets, select a name and get a headquarters.

(ILLUSTRATION FOUR)

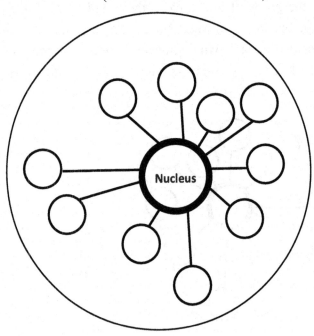

Looking to animals for primitive Meme grouping behaviors, Konrad Lorenz in his work <u>On Aggression</u> (NY: Harcourt Brace Jovanovich, P. 1974 158 - 59), tells of ten rats, assorted sexes, but of the same category, who were put in a cage together by researcher F. Steiniger in the 1940's. After a few days of being frightened of each other, one male and one female tied the knot. This union, a mini-Meme, brought out their aggression and they terrorized and murdered all the other rats. This is a perfect example of Matriarchal and Patriarchal power in formation, the natural building blocks of a Human Family Meme.

Understand, however, Memes are unstable, they have no physical structure, nevertheless, they do exist and, as in any other cell, organic or social, they are structured according to natural law. Additionally, never forget, Memes are mental formations (Mental Models) expanded to draw from many brains. Therefore, it stands to reason they would pattern themselves like all cells do.

Thinking of a Meme as a globally shaped, three dimensional sphere, more or less the same as any other physical cell, is helpful. A Meme would, necessarily, sport a nuclei or center, then material of lesser and lesser matter (commitment) leading to an outer shell (barrier).

Person's accepted inside this shell (Social Organism), even those near the outer fringe, such as the perpetually poor, are "Memed-in;" those outside are "Memed-out." Often this designation is made official, such as in political organisms (countries). The "ins" are "citizens," the "outs" are "refugees, immigrants, and aliens, often illegal!"

Upon being accepted into a Meme (Memeing-in), even as an alien, one then becomes a "legal" alien, "a green card holder" and/or a visa holder. If one is not "legal," then even if one's body is living deep in the organism's boarders, they are still an outsider or "Memed-out." At this level, these seekers have little or no rights or privileges and no say over

51

the outcome of the meme's actions. Enough outsiders, with no method of being heard, is the major cause of revolution.

This is what happened, gradually, to the Roman Empire. Over the final 150 years of its existence, the Aristocrats (Rulers) and their Cadre' of the civil government pulled away, often moving to the countryside. Simultaneously, hordes of refugees moved in, but they had no idea how to run the place. Today we talk of the "Barbarian Invasions," but, in reality, they were little different than our Middle Easterners flooding into Europe today or Latin Americans migrating into the U.S.

From the outer fringe, poor or lowly status, as one interacts with the forces of the Meme, the expectation is that one will migrate ever closer to the center of the organism, depending upon the sacrifice or effort one is prepared to make and/or on the degree of acceptance the "Meme establishment" is prepared to offer. However, as long as the Meme is intact, those at or near the center still control the destiny of the organism as a whole and the lives of the people therein.   True to their name, they are "the establishment."

Now, let's journey from the inside of a Meme to its outside, literally, from President to Peasant.

The Arena of Ideas and Beliefs.

At a Meme's core, its nucleus, is the nerve center. In an ant hill, this would be the Queen's chamber. (E. O. Wilson's now famous work observing Ant populations has given social scientists much data to help study human cells as well).

I have named this: the "Arena of Ideas and Beliefs." The reason for this label is to focus on the psychic or mental nature of a Meme, brain-centered, not brawn-based; an organ of thinking and cognition, rather than of reproduction.

Society legitimizes the result of Meme activity by giving it a name, building it a headquarters, planting a flag and drawing dots on a map. But the Meme itself will never exist physically; only its resulting Social Organism can be touched, seen and packaged.

TEN: Meme Law states: While Memes form the structure and platform of every Human Social Organism which gives face and structure to the Meme's concepts and principles, the Meme itself, while the real driving force of the Social Organism, remains invisible and unlocatable.

The USSR, one of the largest Human Social Organisms in history, existed one day, the next it did not. Its Capitol structure, the Kremlin, was in place; so were Moscow and the nation's power grid. Even the Republics (Uzbekistan, Kazakhstan etc.), vital sub-memes were in place as were the Army, Navy, and Universities. But the Rulers and Power Elites at the center walked out and the Arena of Ideas and Beliefs was vacated; thus the meme failed to operate, as Rome had done 1600 years earlier.

In these cases, just as in the case of the Confederate States of America, all fell into a dormant Phantom state. Soon, the USSR's Meme structure adapted, by adopting a formerly abandoned organism covering the same location and population. "Russia" emerged and quite easily began operating as the Russian Federation. After ninety-years of dormancy, thanks to all the markers of the former Meme's existence still being in place: the Russian language, religion and social traditions, and, thanks to this Meme being land-based (on the same landmass as the USSR), the lights were back on and the country was off and running. In Russia's case, new titles were given to the offices of government and most of the same members of leadership simply swung over.

More or less the same thing happened from 1970 through 2013 in America. The Confederate States of America, sitting dormant, as a memory only, in the social halls of Southern churches, was revived after the war and reconstruction now as Jim Crow. For nearly a century (1880 to 1960) it blocked human status and full citizenship for Black Americans and carried out its exclusionary work (Behavior Box) using a faction of southern Democrats known as "Dixiecrats (Belief Box)."

But, after the Civil Rights Act of 1963, rising from the ashes of Jim Crow; a coalition of Ayn Rand's disciples, known as Libertarians, joined with Southern Evangelical Christians, White establishment power groups and the Moral Majority (White majority establishment religion) to form the "Christian Right," eventually forming a political arm: the "Tea Party." Just because an Arena of Ideas and

Beliefs goes dormant or becomes a dwarf organization, does not mean it's gone, it just may exist as a Phantom Meme and, as here, we see the "South has risen again!"

Due to limitations of human societal memory, many Whites today are resentful of the White Privilege advantage saying; "Why don't the minorities get off their duffs and do what "WE" have done." They are either ignorant of the past or unable to understand how human social history evolves. This is what author Rev. Jim Wallace calls "America's Original Sin" in his new book of that title (release 2016).

Once a society is structured, it is nearly impossible to reverse the gains made by one group over another.

The Ruling Class and the Power Elites:

Meme members who deed the greater part of their life energy to the Meme, may receive the right to operate in the arena. These we label the "Ruling Class." In a mini-meme, like a family, this is usually Mom and Dad, but not always. It may be Mom and mother-in-law. In a dysfunctional family, it might be Dad and an outside interest, say work, leaving Mom and the kids out to form a new center, perhaps taking in a boyfriend. In some families, I have worked with, the parents abdicated their parental responsibilities and passed the mantle to one of the teenage children. Whatever the arrangement, even families have a Ruling Class.

In churches and volunteer organizations, the Ruling Class, while usually a patriarch and a matriarch, are not necessarily a male and a female, nor are they always a married couple. Churches are NEVER ruled by a pastor; he/she is an "Intentional Outsider" within the Ruling Class, used by the rulers to exert power throughout the membership. Often, however, in churches the apparent elected rulers, say deacons and elders, are not the real power either, a hidden Power Elite rules the roost, perhaps a paid secretary.

In government Memes, the hidden controller could be a police chief, as in the case of extortion expert Herbert Hoover of the 1930s-60s FBI.

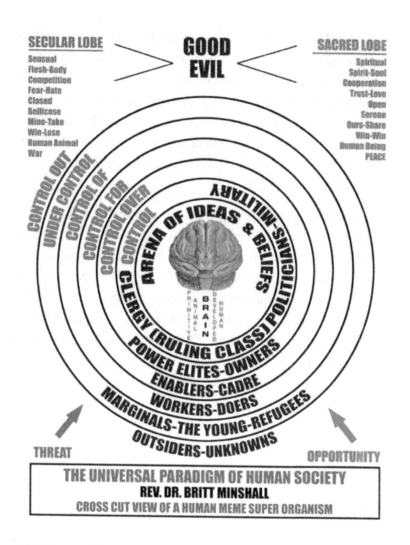

SECULAR LOBE
Sensual
Flesh-Body
Competition
Fear-Hate
Closed
Bellicose
Mine-Take
Win-Lose
Human Animal
War

GOOD
EVIL

SACRED LOBE
Spiritual
Spirit-Soul
Cooperation
Trust-Love
Open
Serene
Ours-Share
Win-Win
Human Being
PEACE

CONTROL OUT
UNDER CONTROL
CONTROL OF
CONTROL FOR
CONTROL OVER
CONTROL

ARENA OF IDEAS & BELIEFS
POLITICIANS-MILITARY
CLERGY (RULING CLASS)
POWER ELITES-OWNERS
ENABLERS-CADRE
WORKERS-DOERS
MARGINALS-THE YOUNG-REFUGEES
OUTSIDERS-UNKNOWNS

PRIMITIVE ANIMAL
BRAIN
DEVELOPED HUMAN

THREAT

OPPORTUNITY

THE UNIVERSAL PARADIGM OF HUMAN SOCIETY
REV. DR. BRITT MINSHALL
CROSS CUT VIEW OF A HUMAN MEME SUPER ORGANISM

DIAGRAM #2

The **"Power Elites,"** who control the rulers, are offstage running the show with a nod of their head or a "no" face, when addressed. In churches the pastor's main role is to take the blame when things go bad and to be fired, so the Meme can get a new start, assuaging the member's conscience and public outcries without changing a thing. In churches, Power Elites are usually one or two long-time, well healed members.

It has been strongly suggested that, in the U.S. leadership structure, the President has actually become a "national pastor." I can see this, in that he/she is and should be an intentional outsider. In reality, the role of U.S. President varies from year to year, depending upon the need of the National Meme. As in a church, the "national Pastor" never really runs the show. But, as we have seen in recent years the President always takes the hit, even if he/she has nothing to do with the adverse situation. Never-the-less, our Chief Executive's main task is to bear the brunt of a National disgrace, yet he/she often gets accolades for something gone well, again, even if they had nothing to do with it.

General Shinseki (Ruling Class), in 2014, was the head of the Veteran's Administration (sub-meme) during a huge scandal involving corruption at the very ruling center of this massively flawed organization. He certainly knew of the corrupt behavior, but was either unwilling or unable to stop it, because of powerful government officials (Power Elites) condoning it to excuse the lack of congressional funding and their lack of commitment to Veterans. At the same time, the inner structure of the VA (Cadre), used the same lying skullduggery to appear to "get the job done."

But, in the end, the General was expected to take the hit, go down in flames if needed and the corruption will go on unabated. What our government can't tell us is 40 Years of "War for Profit" is now backfiring on this good ol' USA Meme. Our bodies are piling up on us and our citizen investors are running from paying the piper.

Corporate life is, ironically the same. While most CEOs do wield power (Ruling Class), "the board" is normally powerless. In most cases, one large shareholder (Power Elite) will control the entire operation using a puppet CEO as an errand runner.

Early in 2014, the Darden Corporation, one of America's most successful operations, bowed to pressure from a major, normally silent shareholder, Brooklyn Capital, a hedge fund, who was dissatisfied with the profits per share, per annum. They were receiving Forty-seven a share as opposed to their target of $63 a share. As a result, over the objection of other shareholders (the board and the management of Darden), Brooklyn demanded Darden spinoff its two oldest and long term profitable companies, the Olive Garden and the Red Lobster (at publication this drama is still unfolding).

This is a perfect example of how the Ruling Class doesn't really rule and how a power holder may be different than most people perceive. In any case, the CEO, like a pastor or a ball coach is one loss from the front door. The journey from "beloved" to "despised" in the Arena of Ideas and

Beliefs is about as long as a train ride from New York to Washington, DC.

In larger Memes, such as a country, as our diagram shows, there are three main forces that make up the Ruling Class: the **Military**, the **Clergy** and the **Politicians**. These, as stated, are not the real power source that is reserved to the Power Elites.

The Ruling Class receives the most notoriety, and sometimes a permanent seat among the Power Elites, but not very often. The best treatment ever of these real world-wide movers and shakers (Power Elites), can be found in David Rothkopf book <u>Superclass: The Global Power Elite and the World they are Making</u> (NY: Farrar, Straus and Giroux 2008).

Big cities like Newark, New Jersey (Formal Meme) are finding themselves in a severe crisis, their schools are in shambles. Hero mayors (Ruling Class) like Cory Booker, a man of the people and enormously popular, gathered together the most powerful, goal centered coalition in history to solve Newark's school problem once and for all.

He enlisted New Jersey's Governor, Chris Christie (Ruling Class but of another political party), along with the power of business, receiving over a hundred-million dollars, as well as onsite support from Facebook's famous founder, Mark Zuckerberg, and fellow Harvard grad, wife Priscilla. They were joined by half a dozen other VERY generous corporate leaders.

Even Oprah Winfrey and President Obama dove into the problem. So there you have it, by far the most powerful leadership team: bi-partisan, citizen-backed, extremely well-funded in history they were a certain win - right?

WRONG!!!!

Why? Because the REAL Power Elites weren't on board. Michelle Rhee, the famed author, when serving as reform School Superintendent in Washington, DC, had the entire Nation in her corner, thanks to a book and a movie about her crusade. Yet, she, like Booker, went down in shambles.

In both cases, the Power Elites in the background, stopping the entire effort, were the teachers and their Union. The money, the businesses, the citizens, the children and the entire nation were on one side, but, sitting silently in the corner, the teachers defeated all the reform programs ("The New Yorker:" "*Schooled*" by Dale Russakoff. NY: May 19, 2014).

Years ago, Jack Welch, then famed CEO, stuck with the task of revitalizing a stagnated General Electric Corporation, ran amuck of GE's REAL Power Elite. In advance of his eight year adventure, he made sure the Board and all the powerful stockholders were on his side. Jack walked the factory floors in a valiant and successful effort to get the Union on his side. Yet, after a two year effort of getting nowhere fast, he wrote of "The Managers from Hell," referring to middle-level managers in the company.

Apparently, over the years, these normally docile leaders remained loyal as Union and Management duked it out, gradually gleaning the real power to themselves. Welch joins Booker, Rhee, really good people in the religious world and righteous leaders in the political realm, in not being able to identify the REAL Power Elites, who, in the end, ruled their worlds. For you fans of Pope Francis' reform efforts, you'll note he has run head first into the Council of Bishops and the bureaucracy of the Curia, who in the end, are the REAL power in the church. Being an excellent politician, however, in his effort to see John XXIII receive sainthood (greatly deserved), he had to also nominate another Pope (undeserved) to satisfy the Power Elites. These are excellent examples of the power of Memes over individuals and Power Elites over Memes.

Just to demonstrate how the Ruling Class is not always vested with power; when a President or Chief Executive (Ruling Class) leaves office, he/she is gone. Many Presidents who leave, admit going into a serious depression the very next day, after their successor takes office. They realize, as Jimmy Carter said in private meetings: "a former president is absolutely useless and completely without power." Carter was right and his statement is also true of former Vice Presidents, Secretaries of State, Attorneys General, state governors, town mayors and business managers. Ex-husbands also fit this category; ex-wives get a reprieve thanks to motherhood, she can't be replaced as the core of the Meme.

This should give us all pause, realizing that these high profilers may never have had the power to begin with.

They were only "loaned" the power for a fleeting moment. These Ruling Class people are, in the best sense, prisoners of their Meme, while the Power Elites control every Meme regardless of its egalitarian nature or claimed power diffusion. You will note that Adolf Hitler, Albert Speer, Joseph Goebbels and Tajo (Ruling Class) are long gone, yet the Volkswagen, Messerschmitt, BMW, Mountbatten and Mitsubishi (Power Elites) families are still going strong.

Of course, this non-vesting of power in one person is extremely good for governance and one only Americans and Europeans seem to totally grasp. Even though it's depressing for the ex-president, downright cruel, it is the reason for the greater stability in western governance.

Assad, Putin, Idi Amin, and Mao Zedong did not have the courage to face that moment of leaving voluntarily. Therefore, their nations are or were stuck with Leaders who became ever more unresponsive. Most have, or will have to use more and more force to retain office, out of fear of being dislodged. When you witness their downfall remember:

ELEVEN: Meme Law states: Members at the ruling power center of a Meme, many with high celebrity status, have no power of their own and are actually prisoners of the Meme, totally subject to the Meme's will as dictated by the Power Elites and the caprice of the populace.

Presidents and dictators, alike, surrender their entire existence to hold their office. It is natural, after making such sacrifices to get and hold an office, to fear giving up the chair - just as it is hard to let a child go, but it must be accomplished. In the Western democracies, with terms limited, Chief Executives actually have their lives saved. If a leader isn't forced to let go by law, the members of the Meme will often kill that leader. Julius Caesar might be alive today, if he were term limited

The greatest gift George Washington gave the United States was "NOT" staying in office. At the same time, it is worth remembering that the vast majority of those new Americans wanted to make him King. This exposes a weakness in Meme structuring:

TWELVE: Meme Law states: In the human propensity to avoid personal accountability, Memes afford the opportunity to shirk responsibility and deed that obligation to others, who will accept the rewards and the punishments. This is the route of authoritarian government and the reason people strain to avoid populace rule, seeking, rather, a professional ruler.

The Cadre:

Those most attached to the established Ruling Class and their Power Elites, "The Cadre," and the general public "Establishment," profit from their place in the structure and desire that the existing structure (Status Quo) not change, so they also work against any alterations. Therefore, the ruler is often forced by the Power Elites and their Cadre to stay in office at the risk of his/her life and that of their children. Assad of Syria, is currently in this position; his life and his family's lives are in grave danger.

If Assad resigns, however, his supporters: Alawites, Christians, Jews and Minorities, will most certainly be slaughtered.

This coterie (Cadre), the next layer out from the ruling heart of the Meme (Ruling Class and Power Elites), is made up of military professionals, business executives, government contractors, upper and mid-level Clergy, the less rich, higher placed civil servants and lesser officials and the under rich, all the way down through local bureaucrats. *The Cadre IS the government and the established power structure.* They make their living out of serving the arena, the rulers and the elites, while keeping the Worker-Doer populations in their place.

In a local rural church, I am familiar with, a church Secretary and the Custodian gathered immense power over the years. These two became the Cadre of two and were family with the church's Power Elites. When a new Pastor was assigned he/she was told at once: "Let's get this straight, we were here when you came, we'll be here when you leave." One pastor complained to the Bishop and, sure enough, six weeks later they were there, as the Pastor said: "good-bye."

In most cases, this group gravitates toward one racial, tribal and/or religious group in society. Once in charge of the Meme, they "crony-up" with each other, sponsor each other and their children to keep tight control over the organism they dominate. This cronyism is at all levels leading to systemic "corruption."

65

Look again at Syria. The "Alawites," a Shiite Muslim minority sect, slowly infiltrated the Meme's core (Syria) that had been for centuries Sunni Muslim controlled." Once inside, they Memed-up, forming a sub-meme with other outsiders and minorities (Jews, Christians and other Muslims and secularists). This syndicate took over the government and the business community and shut the Sunnis out by "croneying" (Memeing-up), just as the Sunnis had done to them for decades.

This group stacked the deck, year after year, to hold the Assad family and their Ruling Class in the Arena of Ideas and Beliefs and they ran the nation dictatorially. The result was rebellion by the Sunni Muslims, who were being disenfranchised (Memed-out), eventually forming a separate Meme - Free Syria. These rebels received their strength and support from Saudi Arabia (Sunni) and the United States (opportunists)

THIRTEEN: Meme Law states: Once a particular group (Tribe, Family or Party) takes control of a Meme, it works to meme-in its own kind of people to operate the Meme to the exclusion of all others; thus the cadre is in solidarity in keeping control of the Meme, eventually consolidating with the position of Power Elite.

This is exactly what happened in Iraq after the Americans left in 2012, which has led to the Middle East blowup of 2014+. The initial conflict came as the U.S. backed, in this case, the SHIITE government of Iraq. However, the SUNNI backed, now phantom sub-meme, called the Sons of Iraq (Saddam's former Army) were left disenfranchised and destitute. Here comes the rescue!

The U.S. invited them to come and fight for us under Free Syria, this time AGAINST the Shiites, to get rid of Assad. But, our effort went bad, the Syrian Sunnis did not want them. So they regrouped under the name ISIS. They then turned on us and began a war against their parent Meme - Iraq (now Shiite). This is DIRECTLY due to the above Meme Law being practiced from 2006 through 2015 and why people, like me, were able to warn of these events futuristically. Ironically, in both cases, it was U.S. interference that caused both countries to collapse to begin with (our same game plan as Haiti, Tunisia, Libya and Egypt.

In America, White Northern and Western European migrants (Irish, English, French, Dutch, German and Scandinavians) formed our Master Meme (National Organism). Black Africans were kidnapped and dragged to America and denied any and all human rights. They were kept in slavery for 150 years (quasi slavery for another 90 years through Jim Crow) and they are responsible for at least a third of the White race's retained legacy, wealth and power to this day.

As later migrants, Eastern and Southern Europeans, came to America, they were allowed into the Establishment and Cadre on a limited basis, in exchange for their pledge to keep Blacks out and serve the country at the lowest levels. "Black" was the Meme marker for "out," anything else was barely acceptable; "White" was the marker for "in." Native

Americans were deliberately "Genocided" from the first day. This Meme alignment remains in place, now simply referred to as "White Privilege."

Historically, as our country grew into a thriving urban culture, three things became apparent: (1) We needed to eliminate the Native Americans (redskin was Memed-out), because we needed their land and, (2) We needed tons of free slave labor (Black skin became inferior), and (3) The poorer new immigrants had to be kept under control, but allowed a place in society: The requirement? To keep their arms lifted and their mouths shut (the "Immigrant" marker became sub-human). They complied.

So, we Americans had perfected the old Roman System of allowing our persecuted to persecute our targets for us. The popularity of this mindset was heard during an August 2015 talk show as a celebrity guest said with sincerity: "If we deport them all, who will clean our toilets?"

FOURTEEN: Meme Law states: The most profitable method of enriching the established Meme members and to keep them safe from newcomers rebelling is to accept small numbers of outsiders to meme-in and offer them a method for achieving insider status by accomplishing a series of unpopular and dangerous tasks.

The best recent example of this rule being played out is in American cities 1960 - now. While Whites abandoned cities in groves the maintained the urban governing power. From the beginning chief bullies like Frank Rizzo in Philadelphia there would "NEVER be a Black cop in

Philadelphia. Only reluctantly did these city armies allow a limited number of Black officers all of whom became the harshest police to their fellow Blacks so as not to get forced out. As a side note, at 19 years of age I was a police candidate in Philadelphia and became a civil rights worker - bye - bye Britt.

Just as Assad, and today's dictators, meme-in certain outsiders, America's forefathers did the same thing from 1720 through America's incorporation in1787. James Logan, an early national political leader from Pennsylvania, and himself Scotch-Irish, invited this practically uncivilized, homeless tribe of Europeans, known for their savagery, over to America with the promise of land.

The Scotch-Irish who answered the call were given rifles and sent to Kentucky and the West, where the established English and German settlers did not want to go. They and their guns were ordered to go west and kill off the Native Americans, so they could have the dead natives' land. (Webb, James. Born Fighting, How the Scotch-Irish Shaped America. NY: Broadway Books 2004). They did a great job "genociding" the American Indian.

Now, earning the reputation as heartless killers, they were seen as extremely good at enforcing rules, even bad ones. So, naturally, southern planters began to hire them as overseers, keeping the Black slaves in line - again, they did a great job.

Finally, as the eastern cities grew, the rulers needed to get control of the street thugs, usually Irish or Scotch-Irish themselves. To wit, our newly minted Police Departments in 1800s America, ordained to keep our underlings under control, fell to this disliked and majorly underclass group - the Irish and Scotch-Irish - again.

For these former "outsiders," this vocational move became the springboard to the developing American Cadre, becoming today's mayors, senators, bureaucrats and even presidents (JFK). To illustrate how slow this process is, the Scotch-Irish arrived in 1730 - Andrew Jackson (1829) was their first presidential offering. The southern Irish arrived in 1840, John Kennedy was their first Presidential offering in 1961. Compare this to Barak Obama, whose ancestors arrived with the first Europeans in the 17th Century; yet, their first President wasn't elected until 2008. But, of course, they were never complete citizens until 1964.

We had learned how to kill two birds with one stone. We let the former Irish street gangs meme-in as "Police" and assign them the task of keeping their lower class brethren, Blacks and other undesirables, under control by beating-up other competing immigrant groups. One day, you're an outlaw street thug; the next, you are the NYC Police Department (Philadelphia, Boston etc.).

These police Memes remain largely Irish to this day. Hopefully, now completely civilized and professional, however all evidence points to the contrary. Forty-four cities were cited by the Justice Department in 2014 for police overreach and brutality.

Hundreds of massive demonstrations across the country by multi-racial protestors, against brutal police behaviors (2014-15), brought the nation to a standstill. I have written for years, trying to expose this Meme-on-Meme violent behavior ("Killer Cops in the American Police State;" For God's Sake newsletter; Renaissance Inst. May 2007 - archived at AllOneFamily.com). It is gratifying to see large, multi-generational multi-racial actions against this social horror.

You will notice, in today's America, an inordinately large number of Latinos are entering the armed services, many not yet citizens. This is a current example of this Meme Law in action.

This process of "cadre enlisting" is the fastest and the easiest way to create a multicultural society. The only problem is, when you need to change things, these now established insiders will almost never give up their new advantage, reacting as any cadre in any established organism will.

When the Egyptian revolution took Mubarak out, Egyptian friends of mine were cheering and partying. I warned them that Mubarak did not run Egypt, it was the cadre-military sub-meme who held the real power; neither Mubarak nor the rebels had any. Additionally, because the general public rebels were ignorant of Meme Law, they did not realize they had to stand-up and take responsibility, in order to earn that power. Mubarak was the symbol of the Ruling Class, a sub-meme member who, remember, like all leaders, was made to be sacrificed.

Workers - Doers:

I label the next group out from the center, the "Worker - Doers." My graph is deceiving in size; as this group should show as 90% of the population (Diagram #2).

Here are the "rank and file" citizens, known from Plato to modern day theorists as the "Producers, Peasants, Workers and the Proletariat." Most of the people reading this book are of this group.

These are the obedient ones, the slumbering masses akin to Pope Francis' "slumbering churches." They send their children to war, their taxes to the government and they obey the law. These are the real stuff of history.

The negative side shows this group is often misused and abused. It is from this group where most of the causalities of war occur. This is the group that loses almost everything when the economy takes a dive. Memes need these people, as their energy source, the heart of Meme strength, more than any other group. Yet, rulers despise and disregard them more than any other group, except the Marginals and Outsiders, who, according to the system hold no value in the scheme of things. That lesser group is only seen when assigned the role of internal enemy and are attacked, first by the Workers-Doers, because, being only one step closer to the center, they fear the Marginals will rise up and the Rulers will make a deal with them for the establishment's place.

Many, from C. S. Lewis to yours truly, have spent a large portion of our lives in order to enlighten the working class

(W-D). Lewis, addressing the average church member (who represents this group), said: "If only the Christian Church and its members would stand against war and injustice the world would see peace and abundance forever" - Alas, he was right.

Enlightenment Christian leaders and academics, responsible for founding modern society, saw the education of leaders and the education of the masses as an antidote to social interclass intolerance and injustice. That's why the Enlightenment Churches founded Swarthmore College, Harvard University, Princeton, Boston University and the University of Chicago.

America's continual problem is, this large group of "the people," enabled by their Enlightenment educations, are still afraid to challenge the rulers of their own Memes, out of fear of LOSING THEIR PLACE in the MEME. Conversely, the Ruling Class and their Power Elite get to their levels because they have conquered their own fears. They understand, to keep control they can use fear of loss to accomplish the task. They realize they need to move forward no matter what the challenge to their plans and threats may be. But, just as fearless as rulers are, the average person, part of the working class, is just that fear-filled. That is why: the workers children die in wars and the rulers' kids live to go to congress. It's not a conspiracy, it's understanding MEME Law.

The Workers-Doers fear for their jobs, lives, their children's well-being and very often, with justification. Rulers at all levels have, since the beginning of time, raped, terrorized, tortured and murdered both their own subjects and those of any other Meme's counted as an obstacle. In 2014 women in India were gang raped on orders of a local court. Torture and mass rape were inflicted on masses of people under Pinochet's rule in Chile, all with a wink and a nod from the U.S. Ruling Class (Pinochet was our boy in Chile). American politicians allow a foreign country great latitude as long as it is in "the interest of the United States."

With their rich benefactor's approval, the U.S. Power Elites, Pinochet and many right-wing Latin American dictators were encouraged in these behaviors seeing themselves as invisible and unaccountable. During this period (1970-2000), alternatively, communism was a step toward putting the working class in charge of their local social organism (developing country).

It did not work; it CANNOT work, because as the people meme-up or meme-in to the organism, it will ALWAYS follow the structure I portray here. Even a "perfect" or perfecting "just" state, will eventually succumb to Meme Law, which, no matter how egalitarian the leaders, will result in class structures. In every Communist Society established during the 20th Century, a superclass of insiders formed up to take dictatorial control, as their Meme formed up and naturally divided the population into the layers of Meme life from the Ruling Class out through the Marginals.

A mass will usually turn into a mob without a ruling center, so no matter what Social Theory states, mass rule without structure can't work because the masses require a hierarchical structure (really spherical like DNA cells with the so called "top" as the "core"). Once established, this hierarchy becomes the Ruling Class and the Power Elites. The fledgling organism soon boasts an administrative Cadre, a Worker-Doer class and comes complete with Marginals and Outsiders waiting to be Memed-out or in. Why? Because it's Meme Law.

Where the United States and Western Europe have prevailed, is in our formal thrust towards a pliable Meme structure under a universal formal set of laws. Also, due to competition at all levels and social mobility (both of which may, unfortunately, destroy the planet and many family lines). Western society is kept in play forcing constant change. This is both the good and the bad.

Marginals - Outsiders:

This brings us to an area our species needs to work on, but which most societies haven't even addressed: the most outside group, the "Marginals" (the young of our Meme) and the new migrants, the "Outsiders." How do we handle those outside the Establishment, who are attempting to "meme-in?" In today's world, as throughout history, this Memeing-in operation is an out and out crisis (Note the Syrian - European refugee disaster 2015+)

Our own Meme's children, we handle differently than outsiders. As for our own, individually we struggle even now to ensure a chance at a solid entry into the larger society. Yet, even as we do this, there are those who attempt to "meme-out" our "own" children and, even more so, the children of the lower socio-economic class.

Meanwhile, many insiders work diligently to exclude new arrivals' kids. "Education," for example, is being used to re-segregate America.

Children of the lesser positioned, usually of a color or language marker, are isolated to underfunded schools, while the "in" crowd (establishment) is complaining that they should not be "their brother's keeper." White establishment school districts across the country spend an average of $5,000 a year more, per pupil, than minority, more urban (Black-Latino-immigrant) districts. Even college is severely divided. Legacy universities especially the University of Chicago, Harvard, and Yale, are gathering places for the international Ruling Class' and Power Elite's children. Even the world's upper level cadre send their children to these famous schools for a sure shot at owning the world.

Marginals' children and lower middle class youth are off to community college to learn to operate the machinery that the rulers supply. This includes the current heavy call for technical and computer skill's education, which is great, but temporary. This field constantly changes, leaving these lesser educated youth constantly caught up in an "in-out-in-out" scenario.

There would be nothing wrong with this if, as it should be, after the sheep skin, only skill and knowledge counted. But, that's NOT the criteria for social success. The diploma from an International Ivy Leaguer or a select state university allows one the networking credentials to attempt entry to the upper levels of social strata (even if you don't make it).

Conversely, Community College actually closes those doors automatically. Then, of course, there is the value of the "network." Only grads from the top twenty can be assured to have the ear of social elites. This is what REALLY determines "who is a big-shot and who will end up as a little spark." Education has become just another Meme Marker along with language and race.

To America's credit, major players of both political parties are putting forth stellar efforts to open the doors of societal leadership to the children of lower socio-economic families. The Ivy Leaguers, such as my Alma Mater, Boston University, along with Columbia and Princeton, are scholar-shipping millions toward gifted young Marginals who could not afford such an opportunity just ten years-ago. Being a big fan of Community Colleges, I am thrilled with the recognition these excellent schools are finally receiving. "Go America! GO!!!!!"

V//: MEME DYNAMICS

Once we become aware of a Meme's structure and its layers of stakeholders, we need to understand the role of these various layers to be able to discern what each member's position adds to the whole. The handicap most of us have, as we "stumble" our way through life, is our tendency to deny or avoid the pressure of the structure with which we deal.

Most people live and die unaware that we're NOT dealing with Joe, Mr. Jones or Mom or Sergeant Smith; we are actually dealing with the Memes they and we are engaged in, respectively: school, neighborhood, family, Marine Corp, etc.. The individuals who seemingly give us so much grief are not isolated persons but are officials in/of a Meme. Literally, they are no longer themselves but role players.

We have already identified the six layers out from the core or the center (the Arena of Ideas and Beliefs), where all major decisions and principles of the Meme are formed. These again are:

1) The Ruling Class (clergy, military, politicians)
2) The Power Elites (The real stakeholders)
3) The Cadre (enablers)
4) The Workers and Doers (producers)
5) The Marginals (the young, legal aliens)
6) The Outsiders (intruders, migrants, illegal aliens)

We now need to discover the primary function of each person within their respective social layer.

Understand, at any one time, most of us are attached to several Memes and hold different positions in each. A Professor of mine, at Boston University, had been the Pastor of the Cathedral of the Midwest, a United Methodist Church, which, in its "heyday" was one of America's richest churches. The membership, some 5,000 strong, was made up of all kinds of people, from all levels of society. But in true Meme fashion, those members, who were the more powerful in business and community, also were chosen as leaders in the church's highest levels (volunteers).

At one time, the Board boasted two CEOs of two of the biggest car companies, serving along with two department store magnates including S.S. Kresge (KMart), a mayor, several state and national Senators - you get the picture. It, however, soon became apparent, that these big time leaders were, in this church setting, extremely docile and completely uninspired. If they found interest in a project they'd simply write a check and then retire from the scene.

In another setting, down the street, a High School janitor was head trustee of another, less prestigious church, where he spearheaded a drive and supervised the building of a million dollar facility. We each exhibit different personalities, depending upon the Meme we are attached to at the moment.

Remember your cousin Robert who enlisted and became Corporal Robert? He was no longer your cousin, if you crossed his path in basic training. Your wife or husband, devoted and true, is no longer the same person if you both become upwardly mobile in the same department. Now, she is your competitor and a Meme loyalist. What you thought was a devoted mate, to win the title of the CFO, will disown you in a second and have you fired, if necessary. Don't feel bad ladies, men have done it for eons. Look at Henry VIII and his eight poor wives. But, for the feminist in the crowd, let us never forget that Isabella, Queen to Edward II, had her husband tortured to death in an unspeakable fashion. So much for the myth of eternal family bliss. Meme Law trumps love at every turn.

When joining a corporate Meme, ambitious people, on their way to the top, will shred a good friend's heart. Likewise, Clergy within a denomination, and military players, will live to support each other, until the Bishop's chair or a pair of "birds" become available. Memes foster competition as their main tool for selecting leaders and insiders. Again, sometimes it's for good, sometimes for bad!

This time, reviewing the "Memeing-in" process, let's begin, not on the insider level, but at the "outsider" level, where many start their journey in the role of "invader, intruder" or, if needed by the rulers, they may become the "tolerated."

Marginals - Outsiders:

In a larger setting, such as a nation, say America, circa twenty-first century, we all know these Outsiders as the "illegals" crossing our boarders. Once inside the physical boundaries of the Social Organism (USA), they, whether legal or illegal, are still "invaders." As long as they are Outsiders, they will never be anything but "intruders." Our recent Presidential election (2016+) argues this point almost exclusively, with MANY candidates vying for the meanest anti-immigrant of all!

Those who are already "Memed-in," the young of the Meme's own (Marginals) and other previously arrived migrants, look at these invaders as a double threat - a danger to "us" and "ours." We mark them as such by name: "wetbacks, Chicanos, rag heads." We also describe their clothing, their eyes, their odors (usually spices they cook with) as other identifiers, to keep them "different and excluded."

We not only label them, but we snarl with disgust, saying words about them to further dehumanize them. Our own Marginals receive a friendlier "smiling" greeting accompanied by greetings of "greenhorn' or 'tender foot" or the "new kid."

Blacks, fresh-up from slavery in America, were treated as outsiders, even though they'd been in the U.S. from day scratch; as long as the Whites. They had been permitted to maintain a physical presence, like an insider, but received all the disgust of a freshly arrived immigrant from elsewhere. Before the Civil War the U.S. Constitution counted slaves as 3/5th human beings each. Many Whites don't realize it but they continue this mindset even today. Worse yet, many Black people have come to believe the rule as fact.

After emancipation, former slaves were given a special pass of "resident outsiders" as long as they obeyed the godless contract terms we Whites offered them: (A) Receive lower than legal wages; (B) Do only menial jobs they will be assigned by whites; (C) Look down and never address a White person face to face; (D) Live only in restricted areas, and (E) Accept whatever the Whites hand down and expect no more.

The election to the White House of a Black President has awakened this White racist monster as never was expected at this time in our national maturity. The popularity of the conservative political movement in America is a refutation of people of color, rising up into the formerly all-White Meme that constitutes the United States of America (98% plus of Tea Partiers are White, mostly militants now WHITE - MIGHT - RIGHT).

Many other long term established "Memers" (Connected Insiders) in the Workers - Doers group do not take to newcomers either. Latinos are to them "spicks," Asians are "slant eyes," Middle Easterners are "rag heads" and the list goes on. In my observations, both as a cop, counselor and minister dealing with all kinds of folks for 60 years, I have found FEAR to be the common denominator, shared among these "xenophobes" (fear of outsiders). This fear probably comes from a sense of their own vulnerability and shaky place in the structure, pushing them to fear and hate the new competitors, out of fear of displacement.

By happenstance and social engineering, America and Western Europe feature an "establishment power base" that is 90% White European or pan-European. Most immigrants, including the 2015 influx, are made up of Middle Easterners and Central Asians. A XENOPHOBIC catastrophe, which has forced Britain out of the E.U.!

Any competition based society (USA) will see more of this than others. Natural Law supporters will tell you that the animal kingdom is fraught with this compete or die competition based on a "survival of the fittest" theme. The age-old question remains "Do we want to base human society on animal behaviors?" However, unlike the old days, when religious superstition ruled, we must now, in the age of science, identify our individual animal traits and their effects on our Meme structures (systemic sin flies no longer), before being able to challenge them.

FIFTEEN: Meme Law states: Competition, as a method of expanding productivity among workers and selecting candidates for Meme leadership, even though fostering interpersonal disputes as the populace battle each other for supremacy, does create wealth which unfortunately, is almost completely driven to the center of the organism, for the benefit of Rulers and Power Elites who foster competition and combat in their continuing quest for wealth acquisition.

Often, hate groups, which are establishment based, use these fears to ignite pogroms and campaigns against outsiders. Most of these groups are funded by a rich person or small group of Elites to benefit their own particular psychopathologies or, more often, their own bottom line. Conversely, the use of fear among minorities and outsiders by unscrupulous business people and politicians, to enrich their own interests, is often employed by those supposedly representing migrants and poor minorities.

These especially evil people use the plight of their charges to enhance their own wealth and power - all the while scaring already fearful established Whites to death to keep the fear burning. In the 1970s, unscrupulous real estate dealers, wanting to "churn" the market, would place a Black family in the middle of a White neighborhood. Then they would infiltrate churches and Synagogues and neighborhood gatherings with warnings of race riots.

The result was Whites listing their homes by the millions - cheap - and rebuying in the suburbs, while home seeking Blacks bought the abandoned "White flight" homes by the millions for big bucks. I do not know if a formal price tag was ever established for this greatest of American business frauds, but it has to be in the double digit billions. It almost single-handedly destroyed America's fine cities (1970-1995) and created a legacy of hate on BOTH sides of the issue that stalks us today.

Revolutionaries, throughout history, are usually Meme insiders who turn on their "own" kind and have reached out through the layers to enlist or gather together outsiders, seen to the rest of the Master Meme as intruders. These "intelligentsia" occasionally offer them a place at the table in exchange for them acting as insurrectionists against the establishment.

Lenin and his Bolsheviks were good examples, as was the entire Russian revolution (1915-18). The revolt's leaders were all from the landed aristocracy (sons and daughters of the rich) and the children of upper level Czarist families. They promised newly arrived outsiders to the cities and very lowly placed Marginals a new deal at the expense of the landed aristocracy and Czarist establishment. The French revolution was a kindred effort. Only the American and Haitian revolutions (1776 and 1805) were not between economic classes, as the French and Russian revolutions were.

This brings us to move closer into the layer of the Marginals, seen by the establishment as "Interlopers; their own - yes, but outsiders not wanted, who are pushing their way in." You'll note on the Meme chart this includes legal refugees and legally welcomed aliens, who are outsiders, allowed just a foothold into the Meme. They are allowed to do chores no one who is "Memed-in" wants to do. In America today it's Central Americans who are permitted to cook and do dishes, cut grass and do formally well paid construction work for a fraction of pre-1996 pay levels.

These persons receive very limited perks and give little problems, as long as they accept the lowliness of their state. American Blacks have been supplanted in this group by Asians and Hispanics, leaving the Blacks, still Memed-out by the color marker, completely unattached.

Europe is facing the same dilemma as the United States, having allowed Turks, Middle Easterners and Islanders from the Americas in as legal immigrants. Now, many native Whites want them gone and want to take those formally unwanted jobs back, but they are hard pressed to do it. This "interloper (intruder) status" is always kept alive among Memers, so these unwanted ones can be asked to leave. Actually, once "in," they won't go willingly.

One major example of a turnabout on this, gave birth to one of the most awful massacres in history. In the 800s A.D., after the Angles and the Saxons were invited to the British Isles, by the establishment Brits, to be workers, they joined with the newly arrived "Red Shanks" (same as the Russians in the east - migrants from Sweden) and butchered their hosts wholesale. Next, the few remaining Brits joined the Angles and butchered the Saxons. Evidently Meme Law NEVER sleeps:

SIXTEEN: Meme Law states: Newcomers to Meme membership are both applauded and exploited by Meme leaders, while the Meme's individual members resent the new arrivals, none-the-less, they take advantage of their newness as well.

Most long-term Memed-in members (say citizens of a nation) only experienced this phenomenon as a new employee or a new member of a family. Remember back to your first few visits to your in-law's house? If you were differently raced or of a different religion or under-educated, you had no doubt, no matter who was saying: "Momsie' and 'Popsie' will love you," that, you were not accepted.

If you ever joined a three or four person office staff like Ann Hathaway did in the movie "The Devil Wears Prada" you've experienced being a Marginal, barely in, but viewed as an interloper in deference to your "beloved predecessor."

You'll note, I've placed the young of the Meme in this category. Most would not do that, but the vast majority of the young in a society, even those of long-term members, especially the lower levels of the Worker-Doers, are nevertheless treated as intruders, albeit with MUCH LESS cruelty than are outsiders.

I have pastored several churches that were peopled by the post-World War II generation. As their own children came up (1960-80) and tried to take "their" place in the family church, their parents gave them a fit. The result, especially among mainline Christians, was the expelling of their own progeny. These churchless young people either gave up attending church or they began and grew the new so called "charismatic" and evangelical revivals (1970-2004), founding thousands of new churches.

My own grandmother (beloved as she was) stood in her kitchen in Boothwyn, PA, some fifty-years back (1957), complaining: "Why should I pay for a new high school to educate "their kids?" She could not fathom that someone before her had paid to educate "her child." In this next generation, as new children of the former outsiders, now the newly "established" come-up, there is a good chance they will have less difficulty because each generation and their children are better Memed-in with more connections.

But, let's never forget the 2012+ effort, by the American establishment, to deport children brought here as infants, never having understood they were illegal aliens. All the while "youngins" who are the offspring of the power established, Ruling Class or Power Elites and their close Cadre, are accepted easily.

SEVENTEEN: Meme Law states: Memes always favor the acceptance of and provide for their established members and their offspring (Marginals), while they discriminate completely against Outsiders and their offspring.

Blood IS indeed thicker than water - it's Meme Law.

Worker - Doers:

Now to the vast majority of any population: "the Workers - Doers. They exist as the "Under Controlled" ones, the most valuable to the Ruling Class. They are kept ignorant of what's happening around them (The Rulers are quick to praise their work, while demonizing those poorer). They are usually extremely cooperative in their assigned role, often acting nearly slave like. In the United States and Western Europe this group is better off than in almost any other country. But even here in America among this group, which represents nearly 86% of the population, they have only 18% of the wealth.

Contrast this to a pure oligarchy like Haiti, where this group represents 96% of the population but has less than 2% of the wealth. In Haiti, as elsewhere, there is almost no middle class to hold their share, so the workers and Doers are compensated as Outsiders and treated as Marginals in their own country. What most do not realize is Haiti's poor are all pan Africans, native to Haiti since the French imported them as slaves. But the 2% of Oligarchs who rule

88

Haiti, are Lebanese Middle Easterners who came to the Island and took over all the assets in 1921.

Ignorance, one of the biggest contributors to Worker-Doers as the "controlled," is the same old furnace firing the rest of societal "fear." As I've said before: "Those who know how to use this fear factor, rule the roost." A perfect example of this manipulated fear at work, is found in the fight for "Affordable Health Care Act in America."

We are told in surveys that 60% of Americans don't want this law. That's because 60% of Americans already have or could easily get health insurance. They are being convinced by the would-be profiteers on healthcare and the politicians that represent them, that if "everyone gets healthcare, you'll not be able to afford yours."

Also, playing into this classist insider vs outsider fear, is the same fear of exclusion that haunts those more Memed-in persons who resist and repress any effort from the Marginals and Outsiders to break into their lifestyle; it's another case of: "If everyone gets a good lifestyle, then I lose my superior advantage over "THEM," who currently are excluded.

Any seeker of the truth needs to remember that even America's religions, that claim to advocate for the Marginals and Outsiders of society, actually support the "Doer" population and everyone in society who are already vested with the best Health Care regimens available.

This explains why "the church" did not open its mouth to support this law, even though it fits squarely into all religious theology. They ignore the precept that the Creator is no "respecter of persons," (sees all as equal), that is to basic needs which everyone has the right to receive, regardless of ones status in life. If this is such a basic tenet of all faiths, then where was the church during the fight for this basic human need (shame again). Yet, there was not a word of support spoken by our religions for Universal Health Care.

We should explain, virtually "all clergy" (Christian, Jewish, Muslim) in America receive healthcare through their denominational group insurance. Also, the vast majority of "churched" people are better off than the bottom third of society, thus they are more heavily insured than poorer people who may need the most help in getting heath care.

Being a follower of Jesus, I can say without reservation, that the teachings of his scriptures and the established historical theology of the Christian Church, have been violated by the American church in ALL settings along with the society in general in not supporting "Health Care for All."

The biggest violation to Christian and other prophetic teachings came from those "already taken care of; who supported their churches' or synagogue's effort to deny those "neighbors," less blest than they. As to the "fear mongering" politicians supported by so many of these "fine establishment types," they're only doing their job, being supported by the establishment who voted to have healthcare defeated. For clarification I need to confess, I joined the Health Care for All movement, not when Obama picked it up, but way back in 1976 when our now President was twelve-years old. My 45-year active membership had nothing to do with partisan politics.

It shouldn't surprise us, remembering in prior ages of the American Meme, when virtually EVERY stakeholder in U.S. society was an active church or synagogue member; in an era when most of the people of earth decided they wanted to live together in peace (1946 +); that not a single American religion (Christian, Jewish, Islam) actively supported the United Nations. As a point of history, for decades many have continued to vilify this world organization at every turn. In contrast many of the earth's religions actively promote war, as an everyday part of their religious message.

The Workers-Doers, with all their power in numbers, simply cow down, as the grim reaper (the rulers of most societies) roam their streets terrorizing them, stealing their children, robbing them blind and profiting from their misfortune. They huddle in fear and often empower their tormentors, if not personally, always through the Religious and Cultural Memes to which they belong.

Too often, we fail to give the German people and their churches proper attention for their near blind support for the Nazis of Hitler's era. We ignore the fact that Hitler was a "big time" hero of the German people and all but 40 churches, out of 5000, supported him right to the 1945 end. We, as Humans, are hard pressed to realize that it's not the Hitler's of this world that ruin it for all, but it is "us," the

Workers-Doers, the common people, that support the Rulers that instigate such evil. We give them our blessing by our silent obedience (even when we KNOW, darn well, our country's actions are wrong).

EIGHTEEN: Meme Law states: Meme members are inordinately loyal to their Meme. Once they are Memed-in or up they tend not to leave from external pressures, but only from internal forces and will defend their Meme to the death, even if they know their Memes position is incorrect.

Cadre - Enablers:

We now move even closer to the center of our diagram and enter the territory of the "cadre" or enablers of the Meme. These are the "interpreters" of the edicts of the implementers, the directions of the most powerful people in a society. They are employed by the ruling class to carry-out the laws and instructions of the Power Elites and the Ruling Class, and in such a role, many times they have great discretion in their enforcement.

This discretion is the heart of "corruption." It is those with the greatest options who usually have the opportunity to be the most corrupt and the most dangerous. Throughout most of the underdeveloped world, order is kept by a professional police, a quasi-military class, usually named "Security Forces (Cadre)." Most are drastically underpaid and are encouraged to get their needs met by extortion and torture of the population under their "protection."

In America, Police personnel can choose between" fair and professional" treatment of citizens or act out as is happening in many American cities, as "thugs and warriors." The lower on the socio-economic ladder one finds oneself, the more easily you are terrorized by government officials wanting to relieve you of all you have, balancing their budgets with your blood (Ferguson, MO).

In some places, like China, there is an unwritten code that allows police and private guards to lock someone away, often in public view, until the victim gives in or gives up. In China, as in America, Police are conditioned to treat the wealthy and the establishment one way, while encouraging a hired "goon" status to their behaviors with poorer classes of people.

The Cadre is a broad term that, at its outermost levels, hosts dog catchers, street cleaners and clerks. These folks aren't usually impactful, except for their part in a network of workers who support and communicate with each other. This group is infamous for blocking those more outside than themselves from contact with higher officials.

For example, in Haiti, until 1992, there was a shadow secret police force, the "Tonton Macoute" (the good uncle). This small band of SS type citizens were part of Papa and Baby Doc's (dictators) goon squad. It was their task to neutralize anyone who questioned the government. They received most of their "tips" from informants who were part of the cadre's lower level government supporters: pastors, sanitation people and local cops, who, hoping to gain approval and move up, would turn on their neighbors, their own children and their "best friends." This is a perfect example of people being Memed-up, losing all sense of a personal life; the more Memed-up one is, the more sold out to the organism one will be.

The same was true in the Shah's Iran, Mubarak's Egypt and is in every other, not fully democratic nation, on earth to this day. But, before we Americans get our hind quarters too high in the air with false pride; growing up during the McCarthy era, I personally witnessed all kinds of local people "ratting" on family and friends, identifying them as "reds." Then, after the accused failed from social banishment, others gathered around to take their houses cheap or get a government job more easily.

It's hard to imagine that, just 60 years-ago, this inner-meme tendency to pit one player against another, could have been so strong, that thousands of GOOD citizens lost their professions and, a few, their lives, at the hands of one rogue "Catholic-Republican, alcoholic politician" who discovered he could manipulate the entire population of the United States with scare tactics. McCarthy, and tyrants everywhere, understood Meme Law and used it effectively.

NINETEEN: Meme Law states: Rulers often pit one Meme member or sub-meme against another, with no rules of fairness or sense of right or wrong; the goal being the ruler's receiving enhanced loyalty from the winners and enrichment from the defeated one's losses. When invoked by the rulers, this process trumps all personal and family loyalties.

In a recent Rwanda war trial, in The Hague, a Hutu man testified that, when the tribal war (Meme vs. Meme) broke out, his best friends were a Tutsi family. As the war erupted, sponsored by Hutu rulers and cadre, he went next door and killed his best friend, his wife and all their children. He "macheted" them to death, willingly. The greatest horror was he was the Godfather to all the dead children.

So far we have focused on lower level cadre. But, as we gravitate to the center of a Meme we discover devoted members with higher rank and more influence.

In a Family Meme, the elevated level of cadre is probably the two daughters-in-law married to the two inheriting sons. In a corporation, we find this group with keys to the "executive men's/ladies room" in upper mid-level management. In the military, you would be addressing full bird colonels up to Major Generals, and in the church Vicars General, Bishops and State Superintendents fill these slots. In the American political governance system, these may be elected, such as newer House members or appointed officials, such as CIA Bureau Chiefs, Cabinet Secretaries or agency chiefs like J. Edger Hoover, who had immense power, even over Presidents.

When these people get the word from the Ruling Class (Arena of Ideas and Beliefs) or directly from the Power Elites, they attempt to institute the ruling to satisfy the hierarchy as best as is possible, although they very often disagree. A case in point would be the Catholic Church's prohibition of birth control. I know many Catholic priests and some Bishops who believe this tenet of the faith to be ill-advised, but being part of the cadre, they don't dare utter a word. Many secretly confide that, "When I make it higher up, I'm going to speak out."

You can guess the outcome. Once they receive their dream job and a big time title, they become even more of a dupe to the system. We think the higher (closer in) we get the better we can change things, but, in reality, regardless of Meme type (business, religious, military, political), the closer we get to the center (top), the more obedient we become, that's why so little ever changes. The system of rewards keeps reinforcing the rising stars, who are more reticent to offer meaningful changes. Interestingly, Pope Francis led others to speak openly indicating certain doctrines were in question. But as the days progress no one uttered a note of dissention and he, himself, is backing off some fresh examinations.

John Kerry, when still a Senator, was a power to be reckoned with and, more or less, a bit of a radical. As his time in the Senate progressed, his establishment self grew over the years. Now, upon becoming Secretary of State, out of necessity, he became obedient to the administration, even if he is in disagreement with the historical John Kerry.

The Syrian Crisis proved that Kerry, generally cautious when it comes to war behaviors, challenged Syria and quickly threatened an attack. Any psychologist could see by his non-verbal's (face, actions, tone), that he was insincere in his own threats, but he was dutiful to the Meme rulers. At this high level (Meme center), everyone in the Meme obeys to the letter. If you do not, it's out with you.

Using Syria as a model, President Assad, personally, is seen by the United States as the problem. Yet, he, like all other rulers, is really a slave to his ruling National Meme. The closer to the power center of any Meme one gets, the less of one's self remains. This is why Assad can't step down. His very life and that of his wife and family depends on his staying.

We have covered this point before, but it cannot be stressed enough, the ruler is the most ruled by his/her Meme, without which, even a former ruler disappears, becoming a non-entity - a persona non grata. That's why most rulers, whose authority goes bad, would rather fight to the death than leave and live. They cannot envision themselves living a life separate from ruler-ship at the center of the Meme. Again, it's much like the Queen ant in the center of the colony. She cannot just pick up and leave. Her enforcers would sting her to death; the ruler is the major prisoner of any Meme.

General Smedley Butler, the most decorated U.S. Marine in history, after WWI, wrote a paper denouncing the cabal of wealth at the top of the U.S. Power Elites, who staged the war to enrich themselves and their Ruling Class. Millions died from 1914-1918, but billions of dollars were made. Butler was slated to be Commandant of the Marine Corp., but in spite of two Congressional Medals of Honor and a twenty-year unblemished career, he was out. He was virtually unremembered until a courageous historian, Bill Huff, of Maryland, lead a decade long crusade to retell Butler's story. The Meme (U.S. Military) to which he belonged at the high end of the Cadre, had tried, with near success, to obliterate him, until this one motivated man stood-up for the truth.

TWENTY: Meme Law states: Meme members can never achieve high enough leadership, even the ultimate office, to successfully challenge the Meme's Operating Philosophy as sanctioned by the power center, without suffering consequences from others in the Meme's leadership and severe reprisals from the Meme's members.

Remember that both School Superintendent Michelle Rhee and her champion Mayor Adrian Fenty, both well qualified and sincere leaders, were ousted by Washington's powerful Teachers Union, while the citizens (lesser in Meme status) of the city stood idly by to watch their schools brought back down.

If you feel major change is necessary, you will face your only options: (1) self-exile, prophesying from the outside, in which case you may make it happen and leave the organism intact, but you'll lose your place inside, or (2) begin a mini-meme to challenge the Operating Philosophy within the master meme, in which case you will end up losing much of the original Meme members. In either case you personally may land-up criminally charged, will be demonized and/or dis-fellowshipped and may end up with an enemy Phantom Meme in your bed.

When attempting to face up to evil, Jonathan Haidt in his famous book, The Righteous Mind (NY: Random House 2012, *p 220*), cautions us to realize: "We the people care more about looking good than truly being good. We lie, cheat and cut ethical corners ... then we use our moral thinking to manage our moral reputations to justify ourselves to others." He goes on to speak of our Genes being selfish and the product of those Genes go on to create like organisms ("Memes" - he did not use the word).

In other words, if one attempts standing for righteousness against any organization, it will cut the advocate to ribbons - then dawn a smiley face, as the champion goes through the grinder. You can take comfort to know, as in St. Francis' and Abraham Lincoln's cases, when dead the righteous champion may be glorified. A similar force plays out in the American custom of naming places for its defeated victims: Pontiac, MI; Cheyanne, WY; Red Skins Stadium; Broken Arrow, OK and Indiana state.

At the beginning of the Obama administration, a promise was made to allow a more open dialog with government employees discovering corruption or illegal activity to speak out and be safe. Now, at the close of that administration, despite the "Whistle Blower Law," these employees are being terrorized by their government, arrested and ruined. This has been a major failure in the American Meme, seeing that even its own civil and criminal laws can't overcome basic Meme Law. You'll note the President's abandonment of his word, while serving to associate himself to the Rulers, has lost him much of his credibility with his supporters, while he put many of his adversaries at ease.

Elijah and Jeremiah of the Hebrew Scriptures, General Butler, Edward Snowden, Jesus and thousands of other "change agents" faced this journey. In my last book, The Jesus Book, I have said that I am honored to be part of this band of outsiders, even though I have not been called to make such giant sacrifices - YET.

Members of the cadre, all levels, find themselves in this most difficult of positions all the time. Their personal choice: be a (1) Corrupted Coward or become a (2) Public Prophet. Keep this group in mind; whatever they decide carries HUGE penalties, not only for us, but also for them.

The Rulers:

Now, onto the role of rulers, who are made up of two separate, but totally intertwined groups. First are the Power Elites, and second is their legates, the Ruling Class. The Power Elites are the "Instigators" in any society. It is their spoken or implied interests that the Ruling Class attempts to satisfy. Power Elites may be well known, such as is Warren Buffet, David Koch, and Bill Gates, or completely in the shadows calling the shots nearly anonymously. In America, and everywhere on earth, these are the folks with the means; they control the jobs, natural resources and wealth of a society.

These positions (Power Elites and Ruling Class) look different, yet are codependent in every organism of society. Let's look at a church I pastored. The Ruling Class was made-up of a Deacon and a powerful trustee. They ruled the church with an iron hand, but the Power Elite ruler, was a quiet, behind the scenes local businessman. He insisted I have lunch with him each month, the day of the church board meeting. He wanted to make sure I knew how he "wanted things to go." He had already touched base with his other two ruling chums, who never crossed him, but always did his bidding.

Every church in the country, congregational or not, is operated much the same way, as are corporate boards. In that setting, the CEO and the Board are the Ruling Class, but large institutional stock holders are the real Power Elites. These Unseen's dictate the Board's every move, often revealed at a private lunch meeting with the CEO or head person.

In a National Meme (Political/Social), the Power Elites spread their influence by where they place their money. They send their children to a small network of schools. Often, they just spread their mind's opinion, which is their right. But, more often, like David and Charles Koch, they simply make money available from the sideline to groups, like the Tea Party, who carry out their wishes.

The highest placed Power Elites of the right support the American Legislative Executive Council, a lobbying group that supports only Republican Legislators at state and national levels and nearly assures their election given their vast wealth. If a legislator disagrees with them, they can guarantee his/her ouster. ALEC is a virtual dictatorship by the American Right's Power Elite over its Ruling Class. Through this mechanism, often-nameless Power Elites engineer the greatest "democracy" to totally ignore the needs of people and enact laws that benefit only the rich and the powerful.

The left has a similar hammer in America's unions, who almost always support Democratic causes. The concern here comes from observers who see the left's support dwindling due to decreased union membership. The outcome is ever growing Right-wing rule and a decreasing influence of the general population in America's civil life.

It is hard to separate the Power Elites from their siblings, the Ruling Class, but, in the interest of scrupulous honesty, we must try.

On TV, we see the Ruling Class at work (West Wing, House of Cards, etc.), however, we only catch a glimpse of the Power Elites in the shadows, where they work with NO accountability, often at a secret lunch or secret meeting on a secluded mountaintop.

Most Power Elites are from wealth; many of the Ruling Class, like Bill Clinton, John Boehner and Harry Reed are not. Many of the Power Elites are legacy holders, that is, they inherited their wealth and privileges. Yet, some from this inheriting group rebel against their legacy and adopt programs for the people, the Roosevelt's, for example.

It may seem weird, but growing up among this American aristocracy, I witnessed, from a very young age, that "old money" was far more eclectic, open, progressive and more sympathetic to peoples' needs than "new" money. Through my growing years, this was a major conversation around the table at the DuPont Country Club.

So, just being labeled the Power Elite does not make you of a particular political ilk. Often, the newest fortunes are the most self-centered, excluding others from their shared background from attaining insider status. The older fortunes (The DuPont's, Weinberg's, Sterling's and the Pew family, along with a thousand others, are the most liberal in sharing their advantage.

The Power Elites sponsor those rising to the Ruling Class, which usually reflects the spread of Power Elite's ideologies. The result is a Ruling Class being chosen by varying ideologies. Some will champion the people (left), while others will champion limited interests, usually connected with business and wealth (right). In today's America (early 21st Century), young industries and a glut of new fortunes are temporarily favoring the right-wing power block; while old money is playing a more hidden role in social endeavors.

TWENTY-ONE: Meme Law states: No matter how widespread the violence of the parties in contention in an inner-meme conflict, it is always either focused on or sponsored by those in the center of the Meme in the Arena of Ideas and Beliefs, with the outer Meme members suffering the greatest consequences.

Always keeping before us Meme Structure, at the center is the Ruling Class, forming the Arena of Ideas and Beliefs, which is made-up of three distinct groups: The Politicians (in America elected), the Military (in America subject to civil authority) and the Clergy. Here, Clergy means the rulers of the varying denominations and should not include the lowest parish ministers or the religious prophets, who, even today, often stand against church and civil rulers, trying to expose the subjugation of the people.

The establishment clergy (all Religions) are usually assigned the societal role of silencing these Social Correctors (Prophetic Speakers), as the "Temple Prophets" (Insiders) did in the case of Elijah, Amos and Jeremiah (Outside Correctors). Sometimes, as in the case of Jesus, John the Baptist and Bishop Romero of San Salvador, hierarchical religious leaders murder them.

The Ruling Class has the duty of being the "implementers," that is to inaugurate programs and institutionalize the will of the Power Elites (some populace centered, some wealth-power centered). In this process, America has done a fairly good job, throughout the Twentieth Century, of balancing moneyed interest with social interest, even though our system tends to act like a pendulum (right - left - right - left ...), which ruins many individuals along the way; usually those in the lower third of society. These "outsiders," having little inside information, usually are the last to be warned of a pendulum swing, which means they get "SLAMMED" because of a late bailout.

The big problem America is suffering from, at the time of the writing of this book, is these two interest modules (left-right) are no longer seeking compromise or common ground, but, rather, one group, actually a mini-meme of the right (much like a revolutionary force in other national Memes), has worked deliberately to disrupt the Master Meme (USA) to get its own way. Even though they claim to be part of the "right," everyone at the right is fearful of them. This hard, radical, right mini-meme acts out punitively against their own party members. They are not willing to "implement," as is their duty, but rather to create: "insurrection!" Other nations are beginning to deal with this same paradigm.

Like a dam in a river, they have disrupted the flow of the Meme force and made the Meme structure vulnerable to collapse. In the end, however, this hullabaloo may do America some good. We had become lazy, just approving compromise after compromise, often not tracking outcomes.

But, traveling through this storm will remake our Meme, to some degree or another. Also, seeing much of the world going through a similar political upheaval, we can appreciate the blessing of a Meme which allows its members to make any complaint they want, even to disparage our leaders. It works like a boiling tea pot, where even the Tea Party can blow off steam instead of revolting.

Discovering the White racist makeup of this right-wing group, ignited by our having an African American President, has actually led to their being discredited by America's rank and file, who did not realize the entire thing was a racial hoax. The good thing is, that America is, FINALLY, looking at its own racist self, with honest introspection and shame. For at least the past fifty-years, I saw the U.S. as "the Great Pretender." We faked our racial inclusiveness. These ugly secrets about us, in emerging, have done our National Meme a world of good.

TWENTY-TWO: Meme Law states: The stated purpose or label given a Meme, may, often, mask another purpose entirely.

This principle also explains the phenomenon of "friendemies," people who act much like your personal friend, but are mean and often destructive to you. I have had this kind of encounter, as have both men and women friends of mine. What's happening is the would-be friend is acting out subordinate to you, in attempting to form a Meme relationship, but, simultaneously, is battling you for superiority. Meme Law principles apply here, even though your arrangement isn't even a Phantom Meme (this is common with employers and business associates). This, also, explains why husbands and wives have difficulty engaging the same friends. The would-be friends come into the foursome as a separate Meme and each meme of two can take in another member (individual) but not another like meme (couple). Yes, very rudimentary, but basic meme behavior.

No matter what takes place in these inner-meme fights, in the end, America, just like every family, clique or group, will settle back into the Meme structure that every meme shares. Who gets Memed-in or Memed-out will change, but the process of Meme making never changes, from the most ancient tribes to the most modern extensive governing structures. Every Meme obeys Meme Law.

TWENTY-THREE: Meme Law states: Regardless of the degree of "inner" Meme disputes, in the end the Meme must achieve Homeostasis (Balance) in order to

continue to exist, otherwise it will rupture, splinter or disintegrate.

From this scenario we receive our ever evolving landscape of social organisms. Religious denominations are a perfect example as every denomination is a break off of at least one other. As you ride through the south you'll pass the First Baptist Church, then the Second Baptist and so on, up to Fourth or Fifth Baptist.

In St Augustine, Florida, there is a special seafood breading invented in Osteen's Restaurant seventy-years ago. Through the years some have left Osteen's and started Barnacle Bills, the Sea House and others. Each new restaurant is a brand new Meme, but all serve the same great breading.

Companies split and re-split; at one time Republicans were Whigs and Southerners were Democrats and, of course, many of us were married two or three times. Meme Law forms up, creates and often destroys, but, then, recreates a new organism to take the old one's place: same laws, "same great breading."

VI//: MEME OPERATING PLATFORMS

Exactly how do Memes function? What forces make them go? Does the ideological basis of a Meme (purpose) alter the dynamic or change Meme Law governing its operation? Are there different sets of laws for each type of Operating Platform?

Let's examine the types of Meme Operating Platforms:

1) **Blood** – Family, Kin, Tribe

2) **Belief** – Religion/Politics

3) **Boldness** - Cause/Crusade/Movements

4) **Badness** - Criminal Enterprises/National Cleptocracies /Thuggeries/Invaders

5) **Business** - Profit Producing Functionary/Commercial Enterprise

6) **Beulah** - Culture Centered /Tied to a specific Land-Location

By determining the main Platform upon which a particular Human Social Organism is built, you can more easily understand the dynamics (forces) that fire the Meme, even though all Memes work on the same principles (Meme Laws), there are still fine nuances. The paths taken in forming-up and performance criteria are different, depending upon the Platform used to classify the Meme.

While some simple Memes are single Platform, that is, they are of one type and operate on one platform, most Memes are somewhat more complex and many are extremely involved. The problem is made worse when two of these more complex organisms collide and both are impacted by their own dogmas and conflicted by the others.

For example the Palestine / Israel conflict. Simple-minded people like to make it a Religious issue, seeing only two separate faiths in conflict. Evangelical Christians, who support the conflict, seeing it as a way to bring Jesus back, see only the Judeo-Christian Bible accounts of the ancient scenario and that's it. They say, "Right or wrong, Israel is our guy." Their end goal, however, is open warfare to inaugurate "The Rapture" and force the "Second Coming."

Conversely, Muslims the world over, see Islam being attacked, so they exclaim: "Destroy Israel!" thus playing into the plans of the Christian fundamentalist hope for all-out warfare.

The simple would say, "There are two Religious Memes (Belief) involved." But there are also two "Beulah" Memes involved (Each side's god married to the same land). Both groups are "married" to the same land, that's the ancient meaning of "Beulah." Each claims that "our" god married this land and both groups believe that, and that's it!

Next, they are both "Business" Memes, both needing one another, but competing with each other. For example, the Israeli boycott of Palestinian goods is allegedly to protect Israel's safety (bombs etc.). But the ban extends, mysteriously, to the flower dealers of Palestine, who are no danger to Israel, but who do sell flowers at half the price of the Israeli farmers. The result is: Israel bans the flower sellers, who in return dig tunnels to bring in their flowers, Israel turns a blind eye, until a provocation occurs and then Israel can come down hard on the tunnels.

Next, this is a "Blood" Meme-based conflict, as these two groups come from differing tribal groupings that were originally the same peoples. However, 2000 years of journeying has driven them apart.

Finally, there is present a Badness Meme. Muslim groups in Iran call for Israel's annihilation, while U.S. World Scripters (imperialist) see Israel as a wedge power to divide the Muslim world in half (Africa from Middle East).

Of course, as in any war setting, Badness Memes, that are criminal enterprises and weapons dealers, masquerading as legitimate enterprise, complicate the conflict even more.

Many national governments are Badness type Memes, little more than "Cleptocracies." These countries are deeply involved in corruption and terrorizing of their national populations, shoving wealth into the treasuries of their oligarchs. Somalia, under the war lords, was a good example. The Rulers raked in the cash, the people spilled the blood!

So, you have just one Meme conflict involving Belief - Business - Blood - Beulah and Badness and the whole thing is backed up by people, around the world, introducing a Boldness Meme. This is to say, the conflict is now a cause or crusade to win, involving people the world over.

TWENTY-FOUR: Meme Law states: The more Platforms (types) a Meme can claim, the more diverse its support and the greater power it can wield. Conversely, the more Platforms involved, the greater the possibility of long-term unresolvable conflict.

Here is where we should explain that every Meme is impacted by two basic forces: (1) **Internal** and (2) **External**. These can be for the benefit of the Meme or to its detriment.

Since a Meme is a mental structure (cognitively formed), rather than a physical one, its internal forces are generated by the thinking processes of its members and supporters (some clandestine). Memes rarely react to stimuli from minds or attitude from outside their inner circle. Often, the membership actually thrives on the deleterious thoughts of outsiders towards actions being perpetrated inside the organism.

Belief-based Memes are the most intransigent. Religion, for example; but, wherever you see the suffix "ism," you have encountered a Belief-based Meme, religious or not (capital "ISM" / Commune "ISM"). In these cases, reason and factual arguments will usually hold little sway on their course, as they emanate from the emotional brain rather than encountering the rational brain (frontal cortex).

Religion, a pure Belief-based organism, is strengthened by external beliefs about it and these Memes actually appear stronger under societal fire. Take the early Christians, for example. After the death of Jesus, first Jews and then Romans persecuted the sect. For two-hundred years the

Meme became stronger and more cohesive, due to the persecution.

Upon becoming Rome's state religion, external threat gone, and receiving thousands of new members, it actually ruined that faith, from which it never completely recovered. Every 60 years, or so, new, "bottom up," very internal forces break from the faith, starting reform movements.

The Master Meme is demonized during the revolt, but most of these upstarts are in time absorbed back into the Master Meme, which, then, regains homeostasis. Religious Orders (Benedictines, Jesuits etc.) came from this process, as do protestant denominations. Both are leftovers from past inner-meme conflicts.

One can see this same obliviousness to outside opinion in today's Middle East conflict. Islam is ripping itself to shreds, as the entire world looks on. The Sunni sect and the Shiite sect hack each other to death with nary a word from inside that structure; while international groups speak out, only to receive distain from inside that faith from both protagonists.

Even normally docile organizations, like the Egyptian Muslim Brotherhood, are changing into militant machines, seemingly from a mysterious outside force (we now know as surrounding warring Memes). So they are now joined at the hip in battle (Shadi Hamid. Temptations of Power. NY: Oxford University Press 2014: *pp. 19-30*)

A current example is found in the U.S. with our struggle with capital punishment. The rest of the western civilized world has long abandoned this practice, so much so that other countries will not sell our country the chemicals to kill our own in protest of us. Memes seldom care what other groups think of them because they react only to their own internal forces.

In spite of this International condemnation, we stagger ahead blithely looking for other ways of carrying out this primitive practice, even to rebirth electrocution rather than repent and change. We did the same with slavery, keeping and defending the practice 40 years after it was outlawed everywhere else (1830-1860).

TWENTY-FIVE: Meme Law states: External pressure from other like kinds of Memes, elicits a combative defensive response from the targeted Meme, which usually requires a punitive response from the correcting Memes to achieve changes in the target Meme's behavior. This principle of other Meme interference, if pushed to the extreme, can be the primary lead-up to war.

Since these External forces are always present in the form of conflict with other like memes, it is vital to the understanding of the human condition to be ever aware of the type of memes with which you are dealing. Business organisms (#5) are always aware of competition, creating the need to adapt and readapt to market forces. Blood (#1) based Memes (Families), that is a matriarch and patriarch centered unit, are often assaulted many times in their partnership by would-be suitors desiring to steal away one or the other.

A perfect example of the Meme Law, above, comes when dealing with a Family Meme (Blood) working with Memes outside the family (schools, Family Services etc.). One can often run into severe resistance when attempting to achieve a corrective action to save a family's children. I have been threatened with violence if my church and I didn't "butt out!" In any Meme, conflicted outsiders are in danger of being "triangled" into becoming "the Beating Boy".

The police and the courts receive the same resistance to outside intervention. In my case, the children went on to become criminals and/or suffered early deaths. In India, an entire government finds itself at risk, finally forced, from outside criticism, to call for the end to routine rape, some of which were ordered by local government officials. The above should help us see that, just because your Meme leaders call you to muster over an "external threat," it may not be a threat at all regardless of the ranting of your leaders.

Keeping in mind that external threats almost never destroy a Meme. The competitor may assault, the lover may woo or the other religion may proselytize the believer, but Meme challengers will not secure victory until some "internal force" pushes the targeted Meme into troubled waters. A real internal threat to a family may be more along the lines of a job calling one member of the Meme, say wife, to another job in a foreign city. Another may be vocational advancement of one member to a level where the spouse cannot find a way in.

Nevertheless, just as "no one is an island," no Meme can last unless it interacts with the world around it. In unhealthy Memes, that may mean total withdrawal from the world. Interaction among healthy Memes brings changes in their Operating Philosophies and each adapts or adopts if necessary. In unhealthy Memes, this interaction is blocked, this will eventually destroy an unhealthy Social Organism. Isolation from the world causes stagnation and if nothing else, the isolated organism will die from lack of fresh bodies (attrition).

The American Amish community is a perfect example of this scenario in a Religious Meme (Belief). An exclusive "Club" in Delaware, an elite body, accepting very limited entry, is another self-exiled group. They have even removed the sign on their building and avoid seeking new members. Once extremely influential in the area's affairs, they are now seen as irrelevant.

TWENTY-SIX: Meme Law states: Closed Memes, more often "Belief - Blood and Beulah" located, seek to restrict membership, which often brings an end to the Meme through attrition. Open Memes, most often "Badness - Business and Boldness located," depend upon large numbers of people to achieve their goal, so these willingly expand membership accordingly.

America's Charismatic churches are the best at Memeing-up or Memeing-in, usually disparate types of members, to make a big successful Master Meme. Often, these normally limited Belief-Based Religious Memes will also include a crusade theology, to go out and convert the world (Boldness). Then, they will operate TV and radio stations, bookstores and even theme parks or working with cruise lines, thus adding a profit Business Meme type. This accounts for their churches that often boast 10,000 to 50,000 members.

Business-based Memes, are, by nature, open and have it the easiest in facing change and accepting new people. It is simple: "You change and adapt or you're gone." External forces, here, are mostly seen as good. Not all businesses stay true to form and the results are disastrous.

In Baltimore, recently, a family bought a famous old, but many years abandoned restaurant. They spent hundreds of thousands on the renovations. They assumed the long ago fame would bring them business, so they waited inside for the public to come. They had shut themselves off from the outside community and they failed.

Political and Religious Memes (countries and churches), which are a combination of Belief and Beulah based Platforms "seem" not to understand that, while it is human nature not to trust other humans, and especially others from other Memes, this mistrust hurts the isolationist meme the most.

In all cases, since like Memes tend towards combat with each other, so also, people that belong otherwise are so identified. This non-trust facilitates combative relationships which have been harvested by political leaders throughout history and are employed by our rulers to muster us off to war (external threat). But also this force is used to conduct pogroms against "foreign" people within one's own society (internal threat).

Jon Butler, in his famous book <u>Awash in a Sea of Faith,</u> (Cambridge, MA. Harvard Univ. Press, 1990) reminds readers that the American Rebellion against Britain was at a dead standstill and nearing failure, when the leaders began enlisting the churches in support of the fight. Without this allegiance, America would be a British Colony today. Without some "god" factor, there is NEVER a victorious ending.

IBM shot itself in the foot back in the 1970s by allowing a sub-dominant, but powerful, sub-meme, its Main Frame Division, to use this xenophobic fear, to engineer an inter departmental fight (internal threat) to persecute and force the closing of its fledging Personal Computer and Software Operations. Prior to the closing of the new PC Division, IBM was the world's leader in the computer industry. Bill Gates, HP and Dell would be unknown today, if it were not for this inner Business Meme fight. IBM nearly went under from this "monstrous" BOOBOO. But, this goes to demonstrate how just two or three people, using Meme Law, can derail a major enterprise with an Internal Threat.

TWENTY-SEVEN: Meme Law states: When a subordinate-meme forms inside a Master Meme, it must be quietly expelled or accommodated, if not, great harm or dissolution will be experienced inside the Master Meme.

Countries are little different from street gangs. They never allow a like kind of meme (another country or nation) to draw near, seeing them as an invader or as a competitor to be squashed (xenophobic response). So it is that we live on a planet where we are infected by "wars and rumors of wars" (New Testament).

REMEMBER: At all levels, Memes meeting other like Memes have a default setting of combat (Meme Law Five). This is the Meme Law that has kept Europe divided and at war with itself for 2000 years. It is also the principle that keeps Europeans shunning and combating against Russians (migrated Swedes) for 1264 of those years. Ignoring this Meme Law may spell doom for the E. U.

TWENTY-EIGHT: Meme Law states: Memes desiring to merge with other Memes, they would normally repel or conquer, in order to survive and thrive, require strong internal leadership to overcome the will of individual members, who normally reject such transplanting of Meme loyalties. This rejection is entirely visceral, caused by organizational DNA, just as our physical bodies reject transplanted organs.

European tribes (countries) used this internal leadership change agent for centuries to attempt to bring the continent to peace. The ruling families were cross-bred and intermarried to accomplish this goal. A German family was brought to England, where they still rule, and one of them, Queen Elizabeth's husband's mother, Grace, was married off to a German, who was then called to be the king of Greece.

"External" forces that affect a Meme may be social standards set by a larger more powerful Meme to which the lesser belongs. Look at the Mormons. Upon founding, one of their most deeply held theological beliefs was polygamy (one husband, many wives). When seeking statehood for their homeland in Utah, the condition set by the American community (Master Meme) was their denomination had to surrender to this outside (external) force and give up polygamy. They did so in what is another case of God changing God's mind?

Interestingly, polygamy among the Mormons rarely existed until their leader was "forced," in mid-life, to accept it, if he wished to continue in the lead. His new bride was 16 years old. The first and older Ms. Young never forgave him, while Brigham thought it a great idea.

Here's a current interesting observation on Mormon Meme beliefs. In June of 2014, the church excommunicated a woman who began an organization to see women ordained to the Priesthood. She was soundly rejected, as was this cause, in EVERY other religion throughout history. Now that she is booted out, her marriage bond is also dissolved and she can't go to heaven - little does the Bishop know! Have you ever noticed that almost all these religious cases of severe descent, involve women? This universality means the "sexist" thing is both an external threat and an internal one.

I personally believe this massive rejection by the religious Memes of the female is because the religious Meme is a female Meme, that is, a Meme dedicated to handling issues relating to the female persona (child rearing, family, morality and the Sacred. Males lean toward Memes that deal with the profane, operative, production and the Secular). So, in this case, the female gendered Meme, ITSELF, rejects and controls out its own gender.

TWENTY-NINE: Meme Law states: Memes may have a tendency to support a gender identity, i.e., MALE or FEMALE, usually determined by the operations of the Meme being gender specific.

The Mormons more easily gave up their probation of Black members after the Civil Rights Act (external threat). Yet, there was another external force also involved in this decision, resulting in the Mormons changing their belief structure. In the past, only 144,000 of them could go to heaven. The addition of their one millionth member called for adjustments to be made. It would appear, nothing is Sacred to a Meme needing to survive, regardless of what god (?) has spoken!"

Let's look at the "Internal" forces that impact a Human Social Organism. In order to understand these social cells, though abstract in nature, and these mysterious internal forces, we need to be aware that all social cells are impacted by the same natural forces that affect physical ones.

THIRTY: Meme Law states: Memes are just as subject to universal scientific principles and physical laws as the rest of the universe.

By way of example:

FIRST: *"For every action there is an opposite and equal reaction."*

SECOND: *Humans social cells (Memes), like physical cells, have the tendency to divide.*

Both of these very basic UNIVERSAL truths work, both with and against each other, to fire the furnace of every Meme on earth, from the smallest family to the largest state. Know these truths and you can pretty well predict future events and understand the world's most intricate developments.

Rulers, throughout all history, have kept these principles before them as they create the paths of history. Ancient Prophets, understanding these basics of human society, were able to predict outcomes with astonishing accuracy.

All through my life, I have witnessed a seemingly mysterious epidemic of war invade the human species. This pathological behavior has kept the West in a killing posture for the past 100 years plus and the East fighting against it for the same period. Armed with this knowledge of the internal Meme forces listed above, those ruling us are able to profit enormously for themselves, even if thousands of us die in the process.

Knowing the External and the Internal Principles of Human Social Organisms has allowed the Western oligarchs (corporations and capitalists), beginning in the early 1800s, to continually control the peoples of Africa and Asia. We, beginning with Churchill, began extracting their natural resources (oil and base metals) by setting them at odds with each other, while western power elites plundered their lands. All the while, millions, on all sides, died in the struggle.

As we touched on before, Tim Weiner, in his famous book Legacy of Ashes, tells the tale of a war weary America and Europe (1945) sitting down to end this meme-combat model of running the world. They began a United Nations to inaugurate a world peace model, based on collaboration and universal respect and prosperity. Their goal was to end war once and for all, an idea that would have halted the U.S. Power Elites plan to dominate the future world.

Thus, an "equal and opposite" reaction to this effort was started in a small group of WWII intelligence leaders and ambitious American Imperialists, Ruling Class would-bees, led by Secretary of State John Foster Dulles (corporate America) and his brother Allan (CIA). They believed that the U.S. would prosper into an Empire, taking the seat of the then defunct European Empires, if we followed some simple Meme Laws. This group of future international "terrorists" met at a home in Georgetown on Sunday evenings (1946-47) to plan programs to counter the Spirit of the United Nations and keep combat alive in search of their goal of world domination.

Their knowledge of Meme Law (remember they never heard the word Meme) led them to form the Central Intelligence Agency's Clandestine Division. Their playbook: the United States would use this service to irritate other nations and inflame others, thus creating enemies and conflict worldwide.

Understanding that like Memes will combat each other as a natural process, the CIA operatives circled the globe fomenting unrest, while other agents backed by establishment, wealthy Americans, fostered "Get us out of the UN!" propaganda. Christian churches in America (subordinate Memes to the establishment, and members of the Ruling Class) either remained silent or most often joined in the anti-UN crusade.

Virtually every time shots were fired or some group from the third world rebelled at the yoke western powers had placed on them, the American establishment and their political-religious arm blamed the United Nations, the Communists and "Evil Empires." While all the time, it was U.S. cloak and daggers creating the havoc and exploiting the former European colonial's dissatisfaction.

This group of fledgling American rulers, although by nature anti-Semitic, backed the planting of Israel, smack-dab in the center of the Middle East, deliberately, to divide the Islamic power Meme left over from the then defunct Ottoman Empire. Understanding Meme Law, they full well knew that resettling hundreds of thousands of "foreigners" (European Jews) and taking millions of acres of land from longtime residents (Palestinians), who had occupied it for 2000 years, would set the Middle East on fire. It's still burning!

At a conference on anti-Semitism in Washington in 2015, many of the panelists were ready to acknowledge the many who try to establish evenhandedness in the world's relationships with Israel (this writer and President Obama), are NOT Israel's enemies. The panel worked to lift the name "Anti-Jewish' or 'Anti-Semitism" from we seeking parity between Israel and Palestine. People who have pointed to the unfairness of the west's dealing with the Palestinian people, continue to be sidelined and labeled as trouble makers. One major publisher refuses to publish anything the slightest bit critical of Israel. I have been caught up in that dragnet with this book.

Within ten years, this CIA clandestine group had indeed set the world on fire, destroying the governments of El Salvador, Venezuela, Iran, Argentina, Indonesia and the entire Middle East. All they had to know was basic Meme Law, introduce certain enablers to the mix, and "voila" nature takes its course!

Naomi Klein, in her earth shaking book, The Shock Doctrine (NY: Henry Holt and Company 2007), actually mirrors Meme Law when putting forth that: the rulers of the west have made the most of this scientific principle of "opposite and equal" reactions to control history. When a Power Center of a Meme understands this principle, they can orchestrate events to elicit an opposite negative reaction to a staged event. Then, by making sure their money is where it is badly needed and very profitable to lend, the manipulators make a fortune, no matter what the disaster.

The UN was nearly destroyed and the American finance, manufacturing and military complex made billions cleaning-up western-staged disasters. President Eisenhower(R) witnessing these events and predicting their future shock impact, but unable to stop them, fell into the disfavor of his own party by warning of the coming danger from this growing sub-meme, which he labeled: "the military –industrial complex."

We have all seen these type scenarios play out in our own communities. In my High School, a little twit of a kid used to run back and forth between two street corners a half block apart. One was where the Black guys hung out, the other was the roost of the White guys. This kid would run up telling a Black guy: "That White guy over there says you stink." He would then run to the Whites telling them: "That big Black kid said: 'F-c- all you Whites.'" You can imagine within two more trips a gang fight would erupt and the "tattle tale instigator" would steal all the best bagged lunches and be gone. This is what Klein correctly purports the U.S. did for twenty-years after WWII. I remind us all "A Leopard does not change its spots; and this same U.S. behavior continues to this very day.

THIRTY-ONE: Meme Law states: Memes, seeking to disrupt the world at peace will work to accentuate the Meme markers of two opposing Memes (race, language, religion), resulting in a Xenophobic backlash and a "Dog Fight" style spontaneous combative relationship.

Another of these Universal basics is that human social cells, like physical ones, keep dividing. This helps explain why Memes are bipolar, just as all people are bipolar to at least a small degree. This bit of Meme Law is a factor responsible for the dynamic, often unpredictable, movement within a Meme. We tend to think that only a small portion of us, who are classified as "clinically depressed," suffer this malady. But, not so! We all struggle with the internal opposition (the other "me"). It's just that some people have a weaker pendulum than others and show more symptoms of vacillation than others.

This division in personality has much to do with the dividing cells idea and it is enhanced by the principle that every action has an equal and opposite action. Even in the beginning of a Human's life, we are both male and female. As we develop, we are at the same instant a selfish grabber and a lovely sharer. As my Mother used to say of me (age 9): "You are a street saint and a house devil" (Mom was a manic depressive).

Also, by understanding the second basic of the ever-dividing Meme with the "for every action there is an equal and opposite reaction," we can understand why, when a Meme is formed, immediately, there will form an opposition to the ruling philosophy and its rulers within the life of the Meme. As a result we can safely say:

THIRTY-TWO: Meme Law states: ALL Memes are bipolar and subject to being ignited by certain triggers, the most usual of which are fear (paranoia), greed and self-interest, any, or all, of which can trigger schizophrenia (internal opposition) and render a Meme unstable and dangerous.

When Memeing-up takes place and a new Human Social Organism is created, even though everyone believes it to be homogenous and in solidarity, splits begin to occur. In other cases, two opposing forces attempt to meme-up to

126

defeat a common foe, but, once that foe is gone, the newly unified partner Memes will turn on each other and often the resulting civil war is worse than the first condition.

A case in point would be Nicaragua and the iron fists of its dictator, Somoza (1936-74).

Both rich business people and poor farmers opposed him, but neither could dislodge him because big time United States interests, United Fruit Company (there's our John Foster [Sec. of State] and Allan Dulles [CIA] brothers), were behind him. President Franklin Roosevelt said of the dictator "He may be a son-of-a-bitch, but he's our son-of-a-bitch" (Penny Lernoux, Cry of the People. NY: Penguin Books 1980 p. 81)

As a result, the poor (Sandinistas) and the business class (Contras) joined forces and they won in a matter of months. However, the blood was not dry on the sidewalks, when these two bedfellows began killing each other. Backed by the United States, the Contras were given guns, paid for by the CIA's sale of drugs on the streets of the United States, in exchange for even cheaper fruit for our markets (See the motion picture "To Kill the Messenger" 2014). The USSR helped the Sandinistas, when the U.S. refused to provide weapons to protect the common people in this fight with their former "friends." Both the USSR and the U.S. were completely responsible for the civil war that followed.

The initial pole of the bipolar occurred when a Master Meme (Nicaragua) had its center taken by dictator Samosa, who then enslaved his people with the help of an external force (The United States). This external force could, then, acquire cheap produce. A second pole (internal), made up of ALL the meme's population, formed a sub-meme and warred against its own center. That is "revolution."

Upon winning that revolt, the sub-meme (now the new Master Meme) formed two opposing poles (Contras – Sandinistas) and civil war broke out. Again, and as always, external forces, again the United States and, later, the USSR, each backed one of the combatants. Thousands died! But, finally, the Meme fell into peace when the population gave up their struggle and the externals backed away. The fact that the USSR was soon to collapse had an impact on the wind down. A political change in the U.S. served the same purpose.

In Nicaragua, in the 1980s, Syria, in 2012, and in Ukraine in 2014, it is the externals that enrage and expand inner-meme violence by pulling the two poles apart and fortifying the opposing forces. The U.S. is a major player in this effort and was responsible for most of the bloodshed in Central America in the 1965-92 era, much like the High School twit that cried: "Fight" and then stole the lunches.

Powerful people had manipulated Meme Law again. I say, "again," because Great Britain, the Dutch, France and Portugal employed this same "divide and conquer" strategy with tribal Memes in India, Rwanda, Indo-China, Burma and the Asian Pacific for two hundred years before the U.S. started playing. Rome invented this "imperious" method 2000 years prior (Timothy Parsons, The Rules of Empire. NY: Oxford University Press 2010).

THIRTY-THREE: Meme Law states: The most effective way to extend control over another Meme is to allow Meme Laws to divide its population into its subdominant parts, then set each at odds with the others and conquer the target Meme, using its own polar opposites to effect its downfall.

One very recent example of a people trying to undo western nation's interference leading up to their colonial takeover, is in Burma (Myanmar). During that postcolonial era and especially over the past ten years, on U.S. and European news, we have heard how these bad guys in Myanmar (the West EMPHASIZES "Burma") need to be replaced. What you weren't told is a hundred years ago, Britain, wishing to control this area, chose one of the four tribes populating this area, the Burmese. They armed them, gave them authority and money and told them to subdue the other three tribes. Once done, the Burmese tribe built their new capital at Rangoon and the members of their tribe became wealthy and powerful.

For decades, the Burmese tribe subjugated the other three tribes, funneling their indigenous wealth off to London. Burma was "good" to the West.

After independence from Britain, the people, as a whole, wanted to better express what the area meant to all the four tribes, so they used their native word for "The Land" (Myanmar), meaning all of the people, instead of the Brits imposed name for one tribe.

However, when Hillary, the "White westerner" visited, "Burma" and not Myanmar. Of course, she, by her nature, a Meme leader, desiring to restore homeostasis back to the western model, had to endorse the Brits' title once again. I'm sure she was unaware of the fact that she betrayed her own call for fair justice, but that's Meme Law.

As in most other cases of Meme Law, this "divide and conquer" also applies to fledgling memes as in personal relationship building. Have you noticed that among three or four friends, one or more are always attempting to drive wedges between the relationships? Usually, that is due to the activist person desiring to control the relationship by isolating the others in the group, one from another. This phenomena infects smaller Memes especially: Families, Churches, Garden Clubs and the like.

Now, to the most prevalent internal force governing Meme dynamics: the natural flow of its members' energies toward the center (usually referred to as the "top," but we avoid "pie slicing" our diagram). Just as natural as high and low pressure areas impact our globe, this inward force is always present and an important dynamic, no matter what kind of Meme we are investigating.

Looking, once again, at the Paradigm of Human Society (Diagram #2- p.48), you'll note that there is a ubiquitous pressure from the outside to gain admittance. Also, just inside the Meme there is like pressure exerted by those most outside the security of the center to push their way into better places ("in" or, more popularly "up").

So, now, we have outsiders, aliens and/or migrants, pushing to get in, while just one step inside, others (the young-refugees), are the poor pushing to get accepted at the table. This pressures the largest group, the worker and doers, usually known to be oblivious of such forces, to animate their own efforts, first to keep the new arrivals out, then to climb closer to the center themselves (more money, job promotions, children to better education). As all these forces converge toward the center, they push the cadre, the first inner circle, interpreters of the society, to respond to this perceived threat.

All members will fight to keep their preferred place by putting down the new comers and by conniving to see themselves promoted to a more inside (privileged) position.

In this process, the Power Elites and Ruling Classes are protecting their positions by promoting their allies among the cadre to more powerful positions. Simultaneously, these elites harvest the energy produced by the struggle of those lower than they. These power holders push the flow of energy back at the people using their own productivity, now placed into the ruler's own coffers, creating ever greater wealth for themselves (this is the very definition of corruption).

The World Bank, under its new President Jim Yong Kim (whom I've met with on three occasions), estimates this upper level corruption in corporations and governments is a 35% reducer in the world's gross wealth index. That means that everyone's earnings from legitimate labor are reduced by a third, thanks to this "skimming" or "syphoning-off" the top.

THIRTY-FOUR: Meme Law states: The more powerful a Meme member becomes, the greater the opportunity and tendency to retain Meme wealth that passes his/her way for personal use. This is a consequence of a leader's requirement to completely surrender to the Meme, therefore, there is a tendency to view the organism's wealth as their personal cache'.

The final step in closing the loop of this dynamic happens when the Ruling Class enacts laws, sets rules or changes moral standards (religious controls). In this way, the rich rulers profit from this "inward-upward" flow of the economic energies and then, they can use the rule of law to push the producers back down and out.

Once the playing field is altered and the smoke clears, the outsiders are still out, the poor and Marginals are just as poor as before, the workers are decidedly worse off than before, lower level cadre are in jail or on the street and the major champions of reform are in prison. All the while, a few very clever players make deals and fly into the inner sanctum, the Arena of Ideas and Beliefs (See "House of Cards" TV series on Netflix for an excellent, albeit fictitious, portrayal of this continuing phenomenon).

THIRTY-FIVE: Meme Law states: The "Arena of Ideas and Beliefs" (Ruling Class) is represented in each society by the three major groups needed to control any organism. In America, and most modern states, the POLITICIANS make the rules, the CLERGY assuage the masses, and assure them the Deity has sanctioned

the Meme's authority and then the MILITARY (including Police) force dissenters into compliance.

It should be noted here, that throughout the modern era, the Academy (educators) have been, to one degree or another, associated with the Clergy among the Ruling Class. Yet, in actuality, they were relegated to a Cadre function, nearly at the lowest level. This was because the Renaissance in educational rebirth (1400s) came from religions who spawned the first Universities. Interestingly, they were simultaneously attempting a defense of superstitious taboos that are the stock in trade of religion. Society is well on its way to disassociating Pastors from Professors and already thinks of the two in completely different ways. But, we still see the academic process as a "salvation" of the world mechanism. This transition must be accomplished to produce a more authentic social model.

In my opinion, the Academy has formed-up in the Arena of Ideas and Beliefs as a fourth power module, which is not sustainable. So, the academy will naturally supersede the Clergy, taking their place in the equation, which may actually save religion by pushing it back among the people. Science is now in the process of replacing the superstitions linked to religion and should always be part of the academy. We need caution, as even now Corporate America is attempting to usurp science with grants and big cash gifts, as they are attempting to do with civil governance, all in the hunt for patent rights and never ending royalties.

In the worst cases, this power process involves war based Power Elites and a Ruling class advocating for combat events, some as foreign wars: Korea, Vietnam, Iraq and Afghanistan; some as internal uprisings: Egypt, Syria, Tunisia and Arab Maghreb (internal to the nations involved).

To all this, other harms done in this "war-violence based model," we must add hundreds of thousands of deaths, dismemberments and ruined generations. And, while this is natural law (survival of the fittest) and normal Meme force flow (Meme dynamics), it is not the dynamic itself that causes the killings. Rather, it's the knowledge of Meme Law and its dynamics (how Memes work) manipulated by unscrupulous, ambitious players (Sociopaths), combined with public apathy and/or ignorance of Meme Law, by the general population that allows us all to join in on the slaughter!

BEGIN SIDEBAR: Actually, this model is ubiquitous across human society. Experiments conducted in a myriad of venues by many researchers, beginning with Richard Savin-Williams, found that meme-up behaviors are nearly "preordained," like "blueprints" in EVERY situation (Howard Bloom. The Lucifer Principle *pp* 91-93).

In one series of experiments, campers, both male and female, chosen at random and unknown to each other, upon meeting, would spend a few minutes getting acquainted. Then, they would "meme-up" one as a LEADER (*Alpha-Authority*), one as a BULLY (*Bata-Enforcer*), one as a NERD (*Gamma-Geek*) and a fourth as a JOKER (*Delta-*

Dunce). Titles in Italics are mine from my seminars - all caps are Bloom's.

Knowing these "gather-up" norms, one can easily see how Memes are organized and structured without plan, but out of need as normal human group behaviors. At the center of a Meme, cascading outwardly, we find three of these positions: *Alpha* LEADERS=Politicians; *Bata* BULLIES=Military & Police; *Gamma* NERDS=Cadre, Clergy and WORKERS-DOERS, 80% of the population. Last is the *Delta* JOKERS= the party guys, the avoid responsibility bunch, also the social drop-outs.

One can find numerous social experiments from professional journals, like "Social Research: An International Quarterly" (The New School, published by Johns Hopkins Press) each of which use different definitions, explanations and titles. They all agree, however, that whenever humans meme-up (gather-up), they will invariably need Leaders and Enforcers to make "it" happen, Nerds to smooth the interaction and Dupes or Jokers to bite the bullet, laugh away the tears and carry out the duties. **END SIDEBAR**.

VII//: MEME MADNESS

In 1852, one of the world's great philosophers wrote a book entitled: <u>Extraordinary Popular Delusions and Madness of Crowds</u>." While Charles Mackay had never heard the word Meme, had never studied group dynamics and even sociology was an unknown discipline, he manages to discuss the mysterious mad behaviors of otherwise rational people within a group or social setting He never knew it, but he wrote the first book on "Meme Madness."

He highlights three major incidents when seemingly rational individuals acted like crazed animals in pursuit of riches.

First, he tells of the "South Seas Incident of 1711," as investors literally shoved millions of pounds (dollars) at those running the trading companies working to establish trade among these newly discovered islands. For nine-years, shares grew by 1700 % (percent) until a single share would buy a house in London. All-the-sudden, the bubble burst as realists discovered, while there was wealth to be had, the price of buying-in had been inflated beyond any possible return. Within days, thousands of people lost their entire fortune, homes, businesses and titles.

Later, in France, the exact same thing happened, as Scotsman, John Law (credited as the real founder of what we call capitalism) sold and resold French citizens on investing in Frances' new territories in the "Membership Scheme of 1717." Year after year, there were actually duels fought over the right to buy stock. At one point, the entire issue was worth about what it would likely be in the 1940s, two-hundred years in the future. If only the investors could have waited.

Unfortunately, they couldn't and soon that bubble also burst and investments worth about $3,000 in today's dollars were worth less than $8 dollars.

The irony, as Mackay reported it, was: these incidents happened after a similar one in 1634's Holland. Here a run on tulip bulbs drove the price of a single bulb from about ten cents to $10,000 in a matter of weeks. People were borrowing on their houses to buy one bulb.

Again, when the correction came, "Tulip Mania" was over in a single weekend. People, in debt for half a million dollars, were left with a dozen bulbs worth ninety-nine cents each.

Before we start pontificating over "their" stupidity, let's not forget America, circa 1929, when the stock shares in corporations became inflated, not because the corporations were worth more, but because the shares themselves were in demand. People paid 3 to 25 to even 500% over value for stocks, until, on a single Tuesday, the market crashed and many stocks worth $1.00, not $500.00, sold again for the proper price - $1.00. Another edition of "millions ruined."

As for our generation, let's never forget 1983: Enron, Tyco, World Com and the "Dot Com" bust. Then came the real estate based crash of 2008. Many readers lost everything in pursuit of a home as a "secure" investment, while some of us became homeless. That too was "Meme Madness!"

Understanding how the human mind works within social Memes, in this last case, my own society, I watched as people begged, borrowed and stole to get cash to buy homes, that, in 1999, were worth $80,000, as they sold for "150 thousand dollars, oops I mean 300 thousand dollars, oh no, there it goes again: 450 thousand dollars!" That's how fast the frenzy was escalating.

As a pastor, I went from house to house, wrote articles of warning and inserted "greed" into my sermons, warning people: "Don't do this!" It was all to no avail. The Meme we call "American Society," including my church and my friends were struck with "Meme Madness."

In private, people would agree with me, they were sensible Individuals. But, when involved in interactions with friends and Family Memes, they "bit the bullet." People, who a month before could not pay their electric bill, were borrowing three, four and five hundred thousand dollars to buy homes that were worth $50,000 just a year prior.

Then, investors were lined-up to offer another mortgage on the same property, so the formerly impoverished couples could purchase a "Condo in Paradise" with no money down. "What luck!" they said: "We went from near homeless to dual property landowners in ten days, with no money down."

Guess what? As in the tulips, three hundred years earlier, in 2008 we also imploded! Meme Madness came home to roost again. Now those $300,000 homes were worth $149,000 and the loans came due. Bank of America stock crashed from $23.00 to $7.70 in one week. The party was over. Unfortunately the goofy pastor who was told to stick to "God stuff" had been right, again. The truth is ALWAYS God's stuff!

Shockingly, it was later revealed by Allen Greenspan, Board Chair of the Federal Reserve, at the time of the meltdown, himself a lifelong member of the powerful, political-economic Meme: Ayn Rand's Objectivist Economics cult, that he: "Never Saw It Coming" ("Foreign Affairs," Nov/ Dec 2013). In the article, he admitted that the crash of 2008 took him "...totally by surprise..."

Following this revelation, Ben Bernanke, his assistant in 2008, later Board Chair himself, said the exact same thing in 2013 interviews. They both admitted, time after time, that this big mistake was shared by most of the "big time economists" of the day, most of which were part of the "Chicago School of Economics," named for the University of Chicago. This faculty was completely sold out to Rand's teachings. I have named this: "Empire Philosophy," they label it "Objectivism." The acknowledgement of "Empire" simply adds a cultural, even theological, component to objectivism (God has chosen US to ...). Here is an excellent case of a "Hidden Meme," not openly participating in, not openly touted, but yet in near total control of an entire nation's economic system.

This is also a perfect example of how even "experts" can be blinded by a "religious" type Meme (Belief-Based Meme) which most of the faculty (Chicago School) and Rand's followers belong to. This Informal Meme, "Empire Philosophy" or doctrine, is not formalized as such anywhere, but it is the backbone of the "Chicago School of Economics." Then and now, this Ayn Rand-powered hidden Informal Meme rides just below the radar, controlling western economics and reflecting Rand's "theory" of objectivism, which was evangelized worldwide by Milton Friedman (CSE) and other Rand disciples. Many of these followers, like other religious people, name their children after their iconic leader Ayn Rand: "Rand" Paul for example.

The thing is, a scientific belief or idea must be proven by mathematical proofs and detailed research. But, in economics, the math is "subjective" and can be manipulated by the practitioners' belief structure. The Chicago School's Meme teaches the principles of: 1): Strength over weakness; that: 2): "Profit justifies anything," and that 3): "humans have NO duty toward one another's wellbeing and are indeed objects to be commodified."

It is, then, natural that two of that Meme's chief disciples, Greenspan and Bernanke, just as in any other religion, had their perceptions, successful as they were, blinded to the facts and evidence, just as most religious people do. Their faith in their Meme was guiding them to avoid reason, which would have been gained by examining all the facts.

I have a close friend, who is well attached to the Hare' Krishna movement. I thought this well-informed "gentle" man and I were on the same page concerning the lunacy of war. Come to discover we are not. He sees war as a necessary part of life, actually supported by his god. In his

Holy Book, the very first teaching involves a good peaceful young man being scolded by Krishna (a Hindu Christ-like being), telling him he should "get up and pick a side in the war and go fight and kill to the best of his ability." Because my friend can't challenge his faith community (Meme) and hold up war as immoral, as it is, he must accept war as a godly thing, even though he knows, it is as evil as hell (pun intended).

The Hindu prescription for doing war continues down through history, trumping the teachings of the founders of each faith. The first Christians (33 - 400 A.D.) held out as long as any. But, once their religion became a state church, even they gave up their antiwar dogma.

THIRTY-SIX: Meme Law states: In order to carry-out any act of high destruction and violence, such as war, the Arena of Ideas and Beliefs must be in total accord - The Political - The Military and The Clergy in complete agreement.

Some may say this is much of what Shankar Vedantam refers to in his 2010 book The Hidden Brain, How our Unconscious Minds Elect Presidents, Control Markets, Wage Wars and Save Our Lives. (NY: Spiegel & Grau). While he never refers to the concept of Memes, he does say that the decisions we make are mostly predetermined by beliefs and standards we unconsciously hold, forcing us to make decisions we think little about.

He is 100% right. I simply add "these Hidden Brain decisions" are grouped in our minds by the Meme process and many are manipulated by the needs of a Meme, rather than for the individual's benefit. The "God and Country" process inherited by most of us from our birth community is fostered, DELIBERATELY, in every nation's war room. So as you sit in your church pew singing and praying for peace, you are actually being primed for war.

Most likely, the greatest volume of these auto-actions (nearly visceral) arise out of family. In a recent case, a 78 year-old father, a good and noble man, found himself in business failure. Rather than just packing it in and retiring, he inadvertently encouraged his entire family and their Family Meme to keep the failing business together. Instead of releasing his kin, who were on the brink of personal failure and bankruptcy themselves, he continued to accept their sacrifice. Remember, this was one of the least selfish people I have ever known. He and his family had no idea the Meme (business) had so taken over their lives.

Who we marry usually depends on who our Father was if we are female. If we are a male, our mother becomes the model - even if you hated your parents. How you handle money is usually the direct result of what you witnessed growing up in your family's environs.

On and on, Vedantam's "Hidden Brain" is really the edicts of the Memes we all serve.

During the 2008 madness, some of us saw differently than the Rand Empire model. We witnessed the same circumstances, but not being part of the Rand Meme, we could conclude a disaster was about to occur. We tried to warn of the madness, but the population had faith in Rand's teachings through their leaders, so they chose to follow her and soon we had madness again.

So, how come people, gathered together in a Meme, lose their intellect and act out as they, as individuals, would never do? One answer is:

THIRTY-SEVEN: Meme Law states: When a person "memes-up" or "in" to a Human Social Organism, they lose their sense of self, safety and faith in empirical data and become a different, often unrecognizable person, depending on the degree to which they surrender to the Meme.

This can be witnessed most easily and is socially seen as good, when young people graduate to one of the most powerful Memes anywhere, their nation's military.

We expect a youngster to join, to follow strict discipline and obey orders. We rarely say it, but the military's main task, is to fight and kill. Please know: "It does not have to be so." I feel it should not be so, but, for now, it is. Personal Note: I, like General Eisenhower, am pro-military but antiwar. With a world full of floods, storms, civil unrest, massive wildfires, earthquakes, plagues and International Law Enforcement needs - WHO NEEDS WARS to fight?

So, let's follow Jack and Jill (a parable). This boy and girl duo comes from Perfectville, USA. They are both religious: Jack - Jewish; Jill - Christian. Both kids have been active church goers, good students and according to their families: "wonderful, gentle, loving children."

According to the Pastor Jones: Jill "would NEVER hurt a soul," Rabbi Smith says the same about Jack.

Yet, in 1969, twenty weeks after High School graduation and fifteen weeks after leaving "Perfectville," Jack and Jill found themselves in Southeast Asia. Jack has fired shots at close range at a family of two women, three children and one very old man. Even though, four of the six died, would we say Jack is a murderer? Of course not. His Meme directed him to do it.

Jill, meanwhile, has fired her first rocket Napalm salvo from her chopper, burning to death three families as they picked rice in a field. The women carried at least four babies in back sacks. Does the fact that we now know Viet Nam was a contrived war by the United States, Jill's Master Meme, lead us to label Jill a murderer? No, of course not. Her Meme called her a hero. Unfortunately, decades later Jack, Jill and hundreds of thousands of their brothers and sisters carry the memories of the people they killed and the horrors they participated in; causing them years of mental anguish.

Tell me "Was Viet Nam worth even one person's life?' I'll answer - "NO!"

When we join a Meme, these are predictable requirements for Memeing-in and the average person tends toward doing most anything, out of fear of punishment, including exclusion or expulsion. As time progresses, the inductee realizes the low guy on the pole is expected to do the ugly work, in order to obtain status as a "good member." Later, as Meme leader, luxury living becomes the reward and one leaves other newcomers behind to do the violent and the ugly.

Back during the Viet Nam War, before America fell in love with being a warrior state, we anti-war types suggested the draft age be raised to 50 years-old. We believed, if "old men" had to go off to war, war would end at once. We were correct. We postulated that only the young and the new will gladly give-up their lives and souls for the Meme, the older ones can then live comfortably off their blood.

THIRTY-EIGHT: Meme Law states: Sacrifices and unpleasant tasks needed by a Meme are assigned to the newcomers and the young members, even to risking their lives; while safe and comfortable duties are carried-out by older, more established members.

This is an excellent time to revisit the stages of a Meme's development. Let's recall the three stages:

Development Stage One: *Phantom Meme.* These confront us constantly. A permanent meme does not exist but, on occasion, two or more people find themselves in agreement on an issue. If Memeing-up does not occur, those joined by a common idea will simply separate and remember that one time, in one place, when two, three or however many were together in harmony on an issue or occasion.

If no action is taken and each goes his/her separate way a Phantom Meme is left in space dormant. Never having actuated, it will soon dissolve. Phantom Memes are not necessarily "Hidden Memes," but often are. Sometimes, those involved continue to activate the precepts of the Meme without being aware of the powerful memory. Once out in the open, the hiddenness disappears, but, if not at all organized, it may still be a phantom in waiting; a flash mob event, for example.

However, if the common issue that drew their minds together is acted upon and a common agreement is held on that action, the phantom grows into:

Development Stage Two: *Informal Meme.* As an example, a few years ago a story appeared that a girl was gang raped in a poolroom attached to a bar in Boston. The gathering of the men and their common desire to have sex with the female instigated the forming of a Stage One Phantom Meme, the lusting, the looks and the shared desire.

An Informal Meme was formed when the males begin to collaborate with each other on how they could force sex on the girl. Once agreement is reached, if some males object and/or leave, the Meme would be abandoned and that would be the end of the process. If however, the group agrees and just one male acts out on the plan, an Informal Meme would be activated.

This action although newsworthy, even to International media, although accountable, is still a temporary organism. Often, these Informal Memes will still have wide ranging effects. Most things we label "Meme Madness" are of this ilk, even though an organization, like the Tulip Growers Guild of Holland (Formal Meme), may be used to foster the activity, the rushing crowd is still an Informal Meme.

In Boston, the madness and the Informal Meme ended as the members went to prison. In Holland, when the market crashed and all were broke, the madness and the Informal Meme died.

This process, of which I suggest each of us must be ever aware, that of "Meme Madness," can occur in seconds, driving a Phantom Meme, non-player, into an Informal Meme, ready to ensnare its occupiers into collective actions, and even, if not intended, can be deadly.

This is what happened in all the manias we discussed. The forces of greed and the specter of getting rich (being satisfied) were brought together. Just as with the sex desire of seven young men, who met one young woman, both the sex and the greed became the catalyst to destroy everyone's life. The population of investors lusting with greed could have walked away from the madness. But, just as the young men, they didn't. Instead, as more minds Memed-in, a sort of synergy raised the fervor exponentially.

When those uninvolved had encountered the stimulus and formed the Phantom Memes (greed and schemes), the second they wrote their checks or planned steps to do the rape they enter into an Informal Meme, "no rules - no regs." They did not know it, but, together, they became the victims of this synergy and being Memed-in, it was now hard to pull away.

The strength of inner-Meme pressure outweighs reason and common sense, making Meme Force the strongest in human existence, the parent of mob violence, police brutality, gang rapes, mass murder and its best friend WAR!

Here's where some groups, relatively few, move into "Formal Memes:"

Development Stage Three: *Formal Meme*. If the actions seeking to be carried out in the Informal Meme are deemed worthy of longevity and the labor to organize is present, then we have on our hands the forming of a Human Social Organism bound together in an action, to be carried out. But, now, we add those missing "rules and regulations." In this case, groups are incorporated, officers selected and operating philosophies written.

A Formal Meme is more exempt from Meme Madness, unless the Meme is self-destructing or becomes infected by a human social virus, say apathy, corruption or violence. Formal Memes do madness all the time, but, as in the case of war, it is justified by planning and strategy and endorsed by the National "deity" through the religious establishment.

Memes are just gathered minds (Phantom Memes), who act out to create informal memes, who then organize to take action. The resulting Formal Meme, then, is a progression from an Informal Meme that goes on to take on a visible structure. It becomes named and legitimized by society, with order and layers of structure. This Formal Meme manifests itself as a Human Social Organism (Free Masonry, General Motors, Republic of Uganda or the Lions Club of Burbank, CA).

A good example of this process would be the revivals in the Appalachian Mountains in the early 1800s. A camp meeting would more or less spring up along the Red River in Kentucky (Phantom Meme). Frontier people, living isolated and primitive, were hungry for collective activity. Civil order and organized society were completely missing from their lives.

As an antidote to loneliness and isolation, they spontaneously flocked to these weeklong camp meetings by the thousands and, instantaneously, an Informal Meme was formed (no order or structure). As the days progressed, experiencing hours of "protracted" preaching, people began to gather collectively into "God fearing families" (Belief-Based) of fellow believers and informal memes became more formalized (imagine those before mentioned cultures on a microscope slide).

By the end of the week, people located near each other, "back home," agreed to meet jointly to work in Formal Memes by creating local churches. Upon arriving home, they did just that, choosing elders, selecting names, locating a building and becoming Human Social Organisms. Many joined with other formalized Memes (meetings), becoming groupings of these independent organisms, forming denominations (Super Memes): the New Light Baptist, the Christian Church and the Cumberland Presbyterian. (Jon Butler. Awash in a Sea of Faith. Cambridge MA: Harvard University Press 1990).

The reverse can happen. After the Civil War, southern society was in ruin. The only things left were Phantom

Memes, like families, political domains, churches and plantations, all left de-funded as former Social Organisms (Formal Memes). Now abandoned they became phantoms. In the 1865 south, these abandoned remnants of southern churches, plantations and a dormant economic system, based solely on slavery, seemed as dead as any in history.

THIRTY-NINE: Meme Law states: Formal Memes are forever. Their structures and outward identifiers (Social Organisms) may disappear, but their force field lies in a phantom state, continuing dormant, awaiting a group with like minds and needs to reinvigorate and rebirth the dormant organism usually with a new name.

As the Civil War phantoms were repopulated, the "South" (Confederacy) chose to reinvigorate their failed slave state, but now as "Jim Crow." Their Phantom Memes: family, church and government, simply reconstituted the former Memes of southern society (cities, counties and states) and rejoined the union, and continued operating, nearly as before, with anti-Black laws in control, minus the word "slavery."

Now, back to the panelists at CSIS (see page eight). Here is the answer to your Moderators opening question about reappearing, "up from the grave:" Resurging movements are born again Memes.

Interestingly, in true Meme survival fashion, the economic need for southern cotton led the North to stop "reconstruction" in its path, leaving southern Blacks, again, to suffer abuse. This abandoning of reconstruction also ignored the fact that nearly 620,000 Union soldiers had died to end this oppression. Little did these heroic soldiers know we would "coward" them out for cotton money!

This is an unpleasant truth about our American society:

FORTY: Meme Law states: Memes are capricious and opportunistic. A Meme will sell-out its faithful, break its contracts and perpetrate mass fraud in order to protect and enrich itself and its members in Power.

Southern neo-slave society, throughout, has been built and rebuilt on the phantoms of the South's churches (CLERGY); the South's plantation system worked through local governments and courts (POLITICAL) and an armed forces unit, Gen. Nathan Forest's Ku Klux Klan - its own militia (MILITARY) and local police and courts. Always, the old phantom was really in charge.

Even after the civil rights movement (1956-70) supposedly crushed this race-based cabal, today's radical right, (same southern entities), joining Rand's "anything for profit" politicians, still impacts American society. Not understanding that "Memes never die," but may lay dormant even for centuries, continues to leave us vulnerable to continual repetition of sick behaviors. We are discovering, reborn Memes can still create "Meme Madness."

VIII//: MY MEME AND ME

In the 2007 movie, "The Interpreter," when Nicole Kidman returns to the UN to kill the visiting President from her nation, Edmund Zuwanee (fictional), who has become a vicious dictator-tyrant, she says "How could someone so good do such evil?"

How could a poor Austrian paper hanger kill over 20 million people? By now, you may be able to answer this question: he didn't! So, then, let's ask: "How could over 69 million, normally, "nice - kind" German people, considered in 1939 to be the best educated, most theologically informed people on earth (There were more churches and Seminaries, per population, in Germany than in any other country on earth), support the killing of millions of people? Does that not beg the question: How could a twenty-one year-old former choirboy, turned U.S. Marine, kill five noncombatant, innocent, unarmed, people, including infants?"

The answer is the same as the rest, the choirboy was joined in his murders by 180 million (contemporary population), usually "good" Americans, just as 66 million "good" Germans (1936) joined Adolf in every atrocity. We've asked these questions before and the answer always remains the same: "Once a person joins a Meme, the more of an insider he/she desires to be, the more that person believes in and desires to be part of the Meme, the more that person is the property of the Meme and will act out as he/she is expected to.

The thing is: **WE ARE THE MEME!** "They" didn't do it: **WE** - as in "**I - ME - YOU**" did it! Until we grasp the concept that this pattern IS: Boom > Bust / Peace > War / Abundance > Poverty / Fear become Dread become Violence...

The universal problem among Humans is that we are cowards, I mean we are real "scaredy-cats!" We are like Spider Monkeys, stealing bananas and running to avoid capture. As Haidt put it in his book: We are "selfish cheaters who only act righteous to look better to society." By the same token, we are terrified to stick our head out of the hole, for fear of getting it cut off and Memes let us get away with all that unaccountability, thus amplifying the threats.

As in military lingo, "Never volunteer for anything!" In the Political Meme insider world: "Keep your trap shut" and among Clergy, "Don't do anything - don't acknowledge any wrong!" because you may step on someone's toes. It's all the same ethic common to all people: "Keep a low profile" and you (personal "I") may survive. Let somebody else save the day or stand for the victim.

During WWII, there was an axiom: *"We saw "them" come for the Jews, but I wasn't a Jew, so I said nothing; they came for the Catholics, but I was Protestant, so I said nothing; they came for the homosexuals, but I was straight, so I said nothing. BUT, then they came for ME and there was nobody left to protest!"*

This is the best definition of the human collective condition - "mass cowardice" - Meme enabled and encouraged! As said before, it's important to remember that the "they," above, was not the Nazis; it was the entire German Nation, who were the killers. The "I" who did nothing to stop the injustice, was just another scared monkey (who, incidentally, got killed in the end anyway).

Today, we've gone a step further. Social media and its complete envelopment of the human being sitting, walking and working allows a person to "zombie" their way through life. Now, we don't have to ignore a human travesty, we never even see it. But Meme Law has produced an antidote to this super-apathy:

FORTY-ONE: Meme Law states: As the populace ignores or cowards-out of its responsibility to the whole of humankind, Celebrities or Prophets, who are powerless, will be generated by the organism to engage the people into the world from which they hide. Rarely, some become leaders, most will be discarded, but, hopefully, some of their corrective efforts survive.

You will note, in addition to unusual hair-dos and galleries of tattoos, celebs, who sit in the Today Show's hot-seat are all extremely involved in various causes. Some, like Brad Pitt and Angelina Jolie work, to a sacrificial level. This is primarily the result of a huge portion of us, who are shirking our responsibility to the whole of society in favor of self-satisfaction. Their divorce shattered me!

FORTY-TWO: Meme Law states: Memes are amoral. A Meme knows nothing of right or wrong, it only knows survival and victory over other like Memes and control of its environment. It does whatever it needs to in order

**to achieve its purpose and that purpose is not seen as
good or bad, but "achieved" or "failed" - win or lose.**

If the organism achieves success, it will celebrate those
who ushered it in and will act gratefully to its members.
With this promise in front of the members, many will throw
their all into the cause of the Meme, even if not asked.

Memes are forgetful and their gratitude wanes rapidly.
Persons, serving Memes for thirty to forty to fifty-years,
once retired are gone and forgotten in days.

**FORTY-THREE: Meme Law states: Memes have short
memories of member's contributions.   Once a Meme
member retires or is removed from participation, they
will soon be forgotten.**

A few years ago, I had occasion to call the Baltimore Board
of Elections Office. I asked to talk to a lady I had known
for some time. She had worked in that office for twenty-
years. Even though there were only fifteen people in that
office, no one remembered her. She had retired the year
before. Like so many others "it was out with the old and in
with the new," an age-old and well-known Meme behavior.

About eight years ago, a thirty-five plus professional career
nurse at a major Maryland Hospital asked me to lunch. The
second we sat down, she began to cry. She informed me
that she had been Head Nurse for ten years. She had poured
her heart into her job and her three hundred staffers. She
threw a big annual party at her large home, and got
personally involved when personal troubles came to one of
"her" nurses. She was even the godmother to many of their

children. In professional circles, she was regarded as "the best" in Maryland.

Nevertheless, a new administrator came to the hospital, "who wanted his own head nurse," so my friend was out. She was broken-hearted, but even more so, when, after a few short weeks, her old friends (staffers) did not return her calls and forgot her completely.

She had discovered a basic fact of living in and serving a Meme: when you're out - you're gone. When one is fired or retired from a Human Social Organism, you are quickly forgotten.

FORTY-FOUR: Meme Law states: A Meme is a here and now, an all-usurping organization that will abandon any and all agreements and solidarity with its members for the benefit of the Meme itself.

Soldiers in America's Revolutionary War were promised a pension. The war ended in 1783. As of 1820, that is forty two-years later, not one penny had been paid to these heroes. During this same post war period the Washington's, the Franklin's and the Jefferson's became enormously wealthy.

The United States government repeated this action after WWI, when the "doughboys" were literally cheated out of their pensions. When these veterans Memed-up in Washington to demonstrate, the government sent in bulldozers and tanks, and with shots firing, they expelled the vets from Washington. Memes easily and regularly forget relationships and promises to their members.

It appears the Veterans Administration is up to this same old behavior, as the 2014 scandals arose concerning fraudulent reports and Veterans dying from lack of treatment, all so a handful of executives could collect a bonus.

America's largest corporations made promises to workers all through the 1960 to 2000 year range, during the great prosperity years, only to renege on their promised pensions and healthcare in 2008, when the economy tanked. Now elderly workers were left flat and destitute. We all stood by and let it happen, because our Meme, in the "here and now," was in trouble and it was easiest to dump the now outsiders and the weak.

When attending college and graduate school, I worked as a janitor for a large Jacksonville Baptist church. Fortunately for writers, janitors see and hear everything.

One evening, just before a church dinner, an elderly lady, Ms. Lee, came to the dining hall. She was anxious to see everyone as she had been in a convalescent home for five months. She sat by the front door, where over 150 people filed in, each making a fuss over her: "Aw,' Miss Lee, we missed you so much, so glad you're back!" They all repeated many variations of the same sentiment.

When everyone was inside, she whispered to the janitor standing silently by (me): "If they missed me so much, why the hell didn't they come see me?" Sorry Miss Lee, memes remember no one unless it aids their bottom line. Yet, the meme wants all of its members' loyalty!

FORTY-FIVE: Meme Law states: Within any Meme, the greatest accolades are reserved for those at the Meme's center past and present, usually ignoring those at the outer levels of Meme life.

Truth is, Meme organisms of any kind are slow to remember workers and volunteers at the lower end of the scale. Interestingly, CEO's and their cohorts, usually the ones who gut the treasury, receive the company's eternal gratitude. The Meme, called "American Capitalism," has little regard for its biggest contributors (workers), only to its Power Elites and Ruling Class players go the trophies.

FORTY-SIX: Meme Law states: Memes are insanely jealous and, while having little regard for their members' welfare, Memes demand every measure of their members' being.

Even casual witnessing of the six o clock TV news, brings hundreds of stories from small towns to large cites of couples and families (Memes all) committing domestic violence right down to, and including, mass murder, rather than allowing a member, husband-wife or perhaps a child, to be shared with an outsider. Often, in such cases, the offended member (victim) is also cheating on the side, but the Meme members have no mercy. Once the members discover a defector, the Meme becomes a vengeful unswerving master, its' members a lynch mob (criminal enterprises such as gangs and patriarchal mid-eastern religious families are well known for these vengeful behaviors).

The same is true of nations. While every nation recruits people to do espionage and spy on other nations, at the same time, these opposing nations (Memes) are spying on the first. In spite of the first nation carrying out an identical program, if the opposing nation's spies are caught, it's off to the gallows. As Meme members celebrate the deaths of these "awful people," they are simultaneously, "praying" for the return of their own "beloved" spies (say 007).

For example, Mr. Phelps (Mission Impossible): "If you or any of your team are caught, the United States will disavow any knowledge of you..." Yes, it's true, if you are an American spy and you get home safely it's a "miracle." Conversely, if you are caught, the USA will not know you. That's Meme Law and it proves true in any country; any vocation.

The astonishing factor to me is that we Humans are devoted to our Memes, full well knowing that most relationships with a Meme will end seeing us cast-off and forgotten. Yet, when asked to give up all of everything, most of us will comply in order to be fully accepted in meme life. Memes demand everything of their members and most of us respond (this is the enabling principle behind war - mass obedience); its why "nice" American and German and Japanese and Arabs have, and will, "kill on command."

It took me decades inside the church to realize, I was not ever going to be accepted as a "clergy" among clergy and denominational leaders. Being a pragmatist, I have always viewed my call as one from God, to serve people, and I worked at it with joy for twenty-eight years. I never regretted the years, many with no pay, and I never surrendered my integrity or my promises for a high office or promotion. I should warn: "If you are an idealist and a righteous person, my path will almost certainly lead to personal integrity, BUT also, professional failure."

Remember, this is not exclusive to Clergy, they're just another power Meme inside a Meme, and total obedience is what is expected of its insiders. Since I did not fit the mold, I was assigned a role as outsider. My Bishop labeled me a "character." Among the clergy class, as in any other profession or political work venue, it's everyone for themselves, but we stroke each other's backs in facing outsiders. Therefore, I was kept at a distance, as are lay people. In business, the workers are separated from the executives, and among politicians, the pros are separated from the electorate.

The same is mostly true across all types of Memes. Those wanting to get the best seats or the center slots must play the game or its life on the streets. Many honest people love life on the street and hate using the "executive" washroom - ditto me!

Another thing one must expect from his/her Meme is arch avoidance.

Baltimore, Maryland had a great Mayor, Sheila Dixon. She did a stupid thing, not really illegal, more irregular; I hope out of ignorance. Big time building contractors give all the politician's gift cards "in bulk," usually $10.00 or so (Baltimore is home to many mega-million dollar building projects at any one time). The assumption (but not the obligation) is that politicians will hand them out as they visit the neighborhoods. It's important to note: that these cards are not listed or reported as campaign gifts, just public relations tokens.

While this process should never have been allowed, for years it was accepted. Most politicians before her had used the cards openly without account.

Ms. Dixon, evidently, had a small bunch of these gift cards, about to expire, left over in her home, so she used some for her own purchases, before they expired, to buy a $60.00 item (+ or -), just the kind of thing the opposing party drools over - even though it was perfectly legal.

She was charged and convicted, by an ambitious new prosecutor (from an opposing Meme), of what was really a non-crime and forced to resign. But that's not our real story.

During her year-long ordeal, all of her former "friends," fellow party members and people close to her turned away and did not know her. Now, nationally famous people including Martin O'Malley, avoided Sheila like the plague following a major tenet of Meme Law.

FORTY-SEVEN: Meme Law states: More powerful Meme members always abandon one of their own in times of trouble, especially one of a lower rank. Lower level members, conversely, tend to blindly support one of their own in trouble, except if the leaders order that person abandoned.

In <u>The Jesus Book</u>, (Baltimore: Renaissance Institute Press 2012) I labeled churches as "households of cowards" a place people go to hide from their faith responsibility to "face-up to and expose evil in society." The problem is Memes avoid risk, pain or harm to themselves. They will expel members who try to push the organism to stand-up for goodness or to expose evil, especially that committed against less powerful insiders and/or outsiders for the benefit of the Meme.

A good example of group cowardice took place recently in Precinct 81, New York City. The New York Police Department was pursuing a policy of "stop and frisk" and arresting any person they came across, in this poorer interethnic area. The idea was to get criminals before they did a crime.

At one time, one out of every four male citizens of this neighborhood was in jail or in the legal system. Most people hauled in were innocent and the officers knew it, but they were pushed by Mayor Bloomberg and their supervisors to "nab" as many people as possible. An unfortunate side effect of the program was, even though most people were released in 24 hours, it soon was obvious that people living in this area could not keep a job because they were repeatedly incarcerated.

One young man, age 31, had been busted 24 times in three years for walking down the street. The good thing was it reduced crime; the bad was, it alienated good citizens from the police. For those witnessing the Baltimore riots in the spring of 2015, it was this exact condition, out of control policing, which caused the entire problem.

In the midst of this nationwide charade, one officer, Adrian Schoolcraft, started complaining to superiors. He was concerned about being forced to arrest people for non-existing crimes: "We don't care if a crime was done, we just arrest everyone," was the commander's response. When Adrian refused to go along, he was threatened by fellow officers with beatings and actually fled the precinct for fear of his life. The police, including fellow officers and "friends," took chase and busted into his home at gun point.

Another famous police "whistle blower" of the 1960s, Frank Scorpio, is aiding Schoolcraft in his current federal suit against the NYPD. Former Mayor Bloomberg, the author of "stop and frisk," forgot one of the great principles of Meme Law:

FORTY-EIGHT: Meme Law states: Meme members given authority to use force on others, will do so exponentially and with little reserve. Having received approval from the Ruling Class, the target could be a close friend or family member, but, in this case, they are just victims.

This is a valuable lesson in Meme Law for everyone expecting their workmates to come to their aid at a time of need. A second principle is equally true, as Mayor Dixon, Officer Schoolcraft, our fired head nurse, pastors being challenged and millions of terminated employees and government "whistleblowers" have learned:

163

FORTY-NINE: Meme Law states: No one in any Meme, including churches, clubs, military and corporations - in ALL Memes, at all levels, is a true friend to any other member. The Meme authority reserves the right to encourage or disallow relations between its members, most of whom will obey the order.

Looking at religion, again, we find a perfect example. Some fundamental faiths will order a family not to speak or have relations with a disobedient member. In these cases, wives and children are not permitted to have anything to do with their father. This practice of "shunning" is kept under lock and key and a big dark secret, of the churches practicing it. Which brings us to another wide spread practice in Meme life:

FIFTY: Meme Law states: The inner workings, failures and disputes within a Meme are seen as "our dirty laundry" and internal secrets, never to be discussed with those outside the Meme.

This principle is widely known among families and small groups, especially not-for-profit gatherings. As a Pastor, I have run head first into this misguided "circle the wagons" ideology for years. It seems that Meme members feel their Meme is the only one (family, church, club or small town) that has suffered an embarrassing happening. The real truth is most of these social organisms have had EXACTLY the same kind of dysfunctions.

At one time, I hosted a gathering called "Prayer and Share." No explanation should be needed, given the title, but the idea was to provide a safe atmosphere for people to "let it all hang out" (the famed John Wesley invented the concept nearly 300 years ago, it became Methodism). Getting people to share their fears and concerns was like pulling teeth.

Then, one night, a very young Black man told of a brother about to be released from the federal penitentiary. He shared of his concern over the release. At once a very proper middle-aged White lady stood to confess her husband was about to be released from the same Federal Penitentiary; a shock since the church did not know she was ever married. Given the spirit of sharing, an elderly White lady stood to confess to the church that 30 years prior, when the church was told her son was in the Army, he had also spent six years in the same Federal Prison.

Just imagine all those months and years of holding that stuff in one's soul. Indeed, Memes are places of big secrets. I used to tell people: "The best thing you can do for the devil (Secular: to make matters worse) is keep your mouth shut, it allows the problem to grow and multiply, causing more damage than it should."

Larger organisms, like governments and businesses, have more difficulty keeping the lid on bad stuff, simply because there are more people involved; giving a greater chance for a whistle blower to come forward. But, never forget, a very large Meme once built an "Iron Curtain" to hide its laundry from the rest of us!

As this book is being penned, another major and world changing exercise in this secrecy statute of Meme Laws is playing out.

After 911, Pres. Bush, Dick Chaney and, my friend, retired Gen. Michael Hayden (NSA and CIA) came together and decided, in lieu of this extraordinary circumstance, to suspend all the rules concerning electronic surveillance on individuals. It became the biggest violation of civil privacy laws in history. But as before, that's not really our story.

I personally see nothing wrong with what they did. Most of my acquaintances, even inside the Washington setting, had thought it had been going on, in a limited setting, before. Now, it was thought to be really necessary.

But, here's the troubling story. Six government employees, at many different levels, in discovering these "secret" surveillances and, knowing them to be illegal, carried their concerns to their bosses - that's what they are supposed to do.

Instead of reacting in a sensible mature way, the employers they reported to, within their respective Memes (Departments), began to harass these honest employees, good American citizens all. Over the next five years they and their families were terrorized by the FBI, illegally arrested and persecuted in a massive police thuggery, much like Officer Schoolcraft (NYPD) had suffered.

Now, the entire charade has come to light, severely damaging the FBI, police officials, President Obama and the entire United States of America. This is the primary reason that when Edward Snowden discovered all the illegal things the government was doing (thousands of violations), even to allies and innocent civilians, he was forced to travel to another country. If he had tried to make things right, while remaining here, it is certain he would have disappeared forever or popped-up dead some Sunday morning.

This tragedy has caused many, like me, to lose faith in our government, including Barack Obama's ability to get us under some kind of moral posture. This failure is not exclusively his, since a majority of America's White population rejects his leadership over the color of his skin.

Here's the real irony: At a Washington meeting (summer 2013), I was sitting next to Gen. Keith Alexander (NSA Chief) when the Snowden case first blew open. He spoke of the WikiLeaks by saying: "We should have just disclosed these programs years ago, most observers have acknowledged that the vast majority of Americans would have approved of the program after 911." The look on his face was totally sincere and he was 100% correct. Why couldn't they have just told the truth? Here's why:

FIFTY-ONE: Meme Law states: Meme leaders tend to elevate themselves and their decisions, thinking them to be sacrosanct and above other Meme members' understanding, which, in turn, adds to their sense of elitism and superiority. As a result, leaders make secret their actions, leading to social rupture, illegal actions and, often, unnecessary internal violence.

Once a member stands up against a bad Meme practice and attempts to correct the wrong, that person is subject to punitive actions by the Meme: silencing, shunning, arrest, discharge and even death.

Many of us have been horribly disappointed over Pres. Obama's abandoning of a major campaign promise for a more open government and protection for whistleblowers. Instead, once inside the "Governing Meme," he became Memed-up with others in the Ruling Class and his administration has prosecuted (better "persecuted") more "do-gooders" than any other administration before it. The Mafia isn't the only Meme that assassinates those who tell all. Religions have done it for centuries.

Remember all those South and Central American Liberationists (Liberation Theology) of the 1970s - 1990s. They are a good example of people run amuck of the "order" of things. Bishop Oscar Romero (assassinated at his altar March 1979) and others were given over to their local dictators by the church.

Haiti's Jean-Bertrand Aristide is another prime example. When the inner-city priest, in the Americas' poorest country, began to champion the poor over the super wealthy, his bishops gave the OK for the oppressors to beat, burn and kill the priest (Jean-Bertrand Aristide. In the Parish of the Poor, NY: Orbis Books, 1990).

When working with any Meme, the challenge is to enjoy the benefits of being part of a Human Social Organism while not running amuck of the Meme structure that supports it. The secret is: "Never become dependent on the

Meme for your life. You will probably never receive what you are promised." Keep in mind, your need will be used by the rulers to subjugate you and other Meme members.

IX//: MULTI-MEMES

Just as "no man is an island" so, also, a Meme does not stand on its own, but is usually attached to and/or layered in with others. Some are subdominant, others coequal and some superior (Super or Master Memes).

Nation-states, particularly, fall into the Master Memes designation, made-up of lesser subdominants posing as one unified entity. The United States has always fallen into this category. Not only did we do it by design (Independent States) but, in our infancy, we allowed two separate economies to exist under our roof. From the beginning, 1787, we almost did not exist because of our great division on slavery versus a free citizenry.

This condition is repeating itself in the 2008-15 era, as political impasses, within differing factions of our population, have paralyzed the government. Interestingly, it's nearly the same Meme demographic (geography and race) that forms today's left (north and urban areas) and right (Southern and rural areas). Remember the principal, a Meme is never destroyed; only abandoned (Phantom Meme), but is always willing to be reconstituted by other minds under a different name at a later date.

The very federal structure of the United States, like China's, containing multiple levels of nearly independent governments, makes both countries "multi-meme" structured organisms from the get-go.

The reason for political instability in Africa, among those emerging nations, is conflicts between subdominant memes (tribes), all straining to be coequal or superior to the others, each using the banner of "nation." But, in Africa, there is no concept of a Master Meme (State) above all others, except in Egypt, which has never been Tribal-Based.

After suffering horribly at the hands of Arab and Indian overlords, as part of Sudan (Master Meme) for years, in 2012 a new nation, run by native Africans (South Sudan), was founded. But, within a year, these once unified peoples began to spiral downward as tribal Memes (subdominant) resurfaced and began warring for primacy (Tribal Memes are the most basic and primitive of Human Social Organisms just up from the Clan, Family or Band stage of Human development).

To illustrate the same forces at work in another setting, abolitionists, like William Lloyd Garrison (1832+), and thousands of others, began to speak out against the practice of slavery. Isaac Newton's law then kicked in, creating an opposite and equal force needed to shape the slave lobby into one force (informal Meme).

The harder the abolitionists pushed, the more the opposition responded with power, until their Meme founded a proper, organized entity (Formal Meme): "the Confederate States of America." After the CSA's defeat in 1865, the Meme went dormant, as we reported before, gradually formalizing its practices into the "Jim Crow operating philosophy" among which its best known subdominants was the Ku Klux Klan.

171

Gradually, post-civil war representatives, from the south elected to the Federal House and Senate, became the Dixie-crats of the Democratic Party, who became a powerful, subdominant meme both of the Democrats and Southern civil society.

After the Civil Rights Laws were enacted, these "good ol' boys" became Republicans, who then joined with other White rural Republicans including Evangelical Christians and Ayn Rand's "anything for profit" crowd and eventually emerged as the Tea Party (Subdominant Meme). However, in both cases Democrat (Dixiecrats 1970) and Republican (today's Tea Party) circles, this same subdominant Meme took over both parties to which they belonged, even though sequentially at differing times.

Even in a well-rounded society like the United States, there exists great distinctions that can be used to cause division. When John Boehner repeatedly said "the American people" he was not speaking of all American citizens, he was speaking for White, mainly rural and southern Americans. That was his constituency.

NOTE: I realize I have spent a large portion of my efforts to document the importance of Meme Behaviors on our lives reexamining the South verses North power conflict and racial undertones in America. Please note: from our founding, right up through today's elections, this inner and inter meme conflict has been, and continues to be the most powerful defining factor in American life. According to any professional sociologist, I have encountered, it will probably continue well through this century. It's just Meme Law playing out! Which brings us to:

FIFTY-TWO: Meme Law states: Within a Master Meme multi-subordinate Memes will generate, some to enhance and support the work of the host's leadership; some to its detriment and even its destruction.

This Meme Law provision can be particularly pernicious if the forming sub-meme is in a position of leadership. The loss of Eric Cantor's nine year speakership and seat in the House was another indication of the effect the Tea Party sub-meme has on the Republican Party (Master Meme). In the Newark School's (Master Meme) scandal, the long term power-holding teachers union (sub-meme) killed the Golden Goose, in that case the children of the city.

A current example of this phenomenon is seen in 2014's Ukraine. Two opposing Memes were thrust together (Ukrainian and Russian peoples). This "union" festered for years awaiting a chance to force itself apart. These two Memes had a long history of combat with each other and never stood a chance at unity; neither will become subdominant to the other.

As the rest of us watched, this case of "human engineering" has mixed two highly intelligent and resourceful tribe groupings together. If part of a greater whole, that would bring spectacular results (USSR). Once cut loose and set at each other's throats, however, the result has been the "cybercrime" capital of the world (High Intellect > No effective Master Meme).

173

SIDEBAR:

This is a perfect spot to highlight the underpinnings of national Memes - TRIBES.

All across the globe, on every continent, except the Americas, Tribes are at the basis of all civilizations. By way of example: in the case of Ukraine, the Russians from Sweden moved in from the north (825 C. E.) to occupy the land at Kiev, their new capital city and the land to the EAST. Already in occupancy, however, to the WEST of the river, were nine tribes of the Polish tribal Meme (Ukrainians). Ever since, these two separate tribal groupings have clashed. The poles won early, thanks to Magyar tribes (originally Central Asian), invading Russia. The Poles then pushed the Rus out of Kiev to a new center at Moscow. It has now been a back and forth tribal fight for 1200 years.

During the soviet era the two groups enjoyed a relatively stable existence. After a break off from the USSR stability has remained to a great degree. Unfortunately, the U.S. and its puppet aggressor, NATO, have sought to challenge the status of Ukraine and its nine tribes and one third Russian residents as "buffer states in order to control the Russians out.

This TRIBAL, naturally-occurring COMBAT factor of Meme Law is used by powerful nations, the world over, to conquer these tribal peoples. The Buffer Zone concept and the breaching of it was the primary lead up to WWII.

END SIDEBAR

In 2013 in Kenya, a tragic mall raid, spawned by terrorists from Somalia, paralyzed the country. The problem in responding was determined to be: "It took way too long to get six men under control." Come to find out the government was working through multi-levels of sub-Memes (Tribes).

Kenya, the Master Meme is really made up of several tribes (sub-memes). Two major tribes are the "Luo," that of President Odinga, and the "Bantu' and 'Kikuya," which speak a different language. In Kenya, as in many other Nations, the Army is made-up of members of the President's Party (Luo tribal sub-meme).

After the call for help went out from the mall, Kenya's Special Police Unit was there in minutes. Within a couple of hours this S.W.A.T. Unit had closed 90% of the mall when, all-the-sudden the President pulled the Police Unit out and brought in the army, HIS army from HIS tribe. Remember, the S.W.A.T. team and police were made- up of people from other than the President's tribes, these were the Bantu, Kikuya and other sub-memes.

The Army was ill-equipped and untrained and totally afraid. The army stood down, allowed the terrorists free range to kill all the hostages and loot the mall. Another example of the ignorance of Meme Law bringing unnecessary death and destruction. President Odinga probably never realized he wasn't making that decision, rather his psyche was automatically operating in "Meme Law, to favor one's own Meme!"

Another, nearly identical case, from a more sophisticated country was in America during 9-11. Then multi-layered sub-memes (FBI, CIA, State Police, Local Police, and others) made 9-11 far worse by hording information or withholding aid out of respect for sub-meme territories. Ten years later, these barriers are still in place and a common radio system has not been installed. Again, Meme Law at work: we keep "Like Memes separate and in competition."

In corporate governance, the same "Meme within a Meme" takes place all the time. About twelve-years ago, any casual shopper at the Home Depot witnessed the company going slowly down the tubes. Even an outside amateur, like me, suspected there was chicanery in the halls of power. Sure enough, it finally came out as a showdown between the Board and the shareholders, who were seeing their stock price plummet.

The Board had closed itself off as a separate sub-meme backing, often blindly, the plans of CEO Robert Nardelli, who was operating, often outside the corporate structure and most certainly to its detriment. In the end, Nardelli was paid a whopping $245 million dollars to leave the Home Depot, which is credited with saving the company.

The Tea Party is evolving into the same kind of "Trojan Horse" for the Republican Party, a 2014 situation I have predicted for three years. As the Republicans struggle for unity during the Presidential election of 2016, it will be interesting to see which REAL Republican Party will emerge the winner.

FIFTY-THREE: Meme Law states: Memes, even if part of the same Master Meme, becoming subdominant, distrust other like Memes, even those sharing the same master and will close down or sabotage each other, if they feel threatened, rather than share for the good of all.

The above is the basis of EVERY civil war.

I have found this especially true among nonprofits, supposedly "out there" doing "good" stuff. I visited Haiti for 11 years (1998-2009), working there with two nonprofit groups, which do not even acknowledge each other. When accidently meeting other International nonprofits working in the country, we barely spoke to each other.

In the mountain town of Kenskoff, I worked with a small mission, whose sole purpose was to take care of totally disabled children, the only one in Haiti. One night, one of our children became severely ill. Next door was the Baptist Mission, a large, well-funded school and care center with a well-equipped infirmary. Our volunteers wheeled the sick child next door for help, but were turned away. It took three hours to get the little one down the mountain to Port-au-Prince to the hospital.

One night in rural Florida, I had a bus full of teenagers on a trip. It was Sunday night. As we passed a country church, one of the teens, a troubled girl, jumped from the bus and ran for the woods. I entered the church explaining what had happened and asking to use the phone to call the State Police (this was prior to cell phones). The church's leaders were visibly annoyed and dismissive, ignoring me completely.

Fortunately, a County Deputy Sheriff from the congregation, came out to help us find the girl. The church never did acknowledge our presence. As we drove away into the Florida jungle, an hour later, we could hear the congregation singing "Since Jesus Came into My Heart."

Unscrupulous people have learned to use this inner-meme rivalry to their advantage. A good example from the 1990's, when education was in a period of flux when teachers were fighting to get recognized and to receive fair wages. At that time, I ran into a now, non-existent organization with a name like "The American Teacher's Empowerment Association." Sounds supportive of teachers, right? WRONG!

The sole purpose of this group was to "reduce" teachers' pay, rid states and districts of health insurance obligations and destroy the teacher's unions. They were for anything BUT empowering and supporting teachers. The real danger is people give money and support to organizations they think are out to do good, when, in fact, these falsely named Memes are hidden and dedicated to doing harm to their wrongly named parent cause.

Many "Healthcare Reform Coalition groups" of the years 2006+ have one purpose only; to completely block any and all health reforms.

So far, in our examination of Multi-memes, we have: sub-memes in larger Memes, abandoned Memes rising again, conflicting Memes reacting to each other and Hidden Memes, many wrongly titled on purpose to "Trojan Horse" their way into a position of doing real damage to their apparent namesake or Master Meme.

Often, in a situation, we find ourselves dealing with interconnected, but often conflicting Memes that place us between "the rock and the hard place." I recall the famous story of a U.S. Naval Admiral. Apparently, during the battle for the Coral Sea in 1942-3. A junior officer fell off the ship he was commanding. When told, the Admiral gave the order "Keep full ahead." "But,' retorted his bridge officer, 'that sailor will surely die!" "You heard me sailor, full ahead," said the Admiral. "But Sir,' responded the bridge officer 'That sailor is your son!"

This kind of dilemma impacts us throughout our lives. Politicians playing their game pride themselves on putting their opponent in such a position: "Oh, what to do?" Family members, especially parents, often unwittingly, engineer their children's future in such a way as to place a particular child in a "damned if you do-damned if you don't" situation.

Business leaders are familiar with this kind of a quandary. Perhaps a product the company makes is unregulated, selling like hotcakes, but a problem is spotted. If the business secretly modifies the product, all remains well, but far less profitable. If not altered and no warning is given, the item can be downright harmful. Recently, a large Ice Cream maker from Texas found itself in this very quandary by ignoring a long-term Listeria infection. The

Meme (business) needs that profit. "Oh, what to do - what to do?"

Many bankers were put in this position from 2000 through 2008. If they got sucked into the derivatives deceit market, they were hailed as successful rich bankers, their stock soared. If they kept their heads and did as they should for their customers, their stock plummeted and they were soon on the street. "Oh what do I do?"

In cases like these, the conflicted Meme's core leaders attempting to do right, found themselves in conflict with other's interests in the Meme: stockholders, customers, SEC ethics teams and, finally, their own personal Family Meme (a spouse at home badgering "we need the money, the hell with ethics") and the exec's own ego and need for success). This is an extreme, but very current case!

But how about those Cops in New York City (and all over the world), who found themselves caught between their police employer (sub-meme), their civic employer (Master Meme), the establishment's fears (Phantom Meme), order centered laws (professional responsibility) and the need to keep their jobs (Family Meme). All this juxtaposed to acting unjustly to an ordinary, usually weaker, innocent citizen and the laws protecting people (Justice - Mercy - Understanding - Kindness and ALL the trappings of the Human Soul). As any person, who has ever found themselves on the persecuted side of the law, even if innocent, will attest, it is a never-ending nightmare.

These intertwined Meme forces, pushing on the individual officer's persona, is what allows individual, hot headed bullies, like Daniel Pantaleo, to choke an Eric Garner to death; as other officers coward-out over Garners cries of "I can't breathe!" In MOST ALL cases where I have witnessed or investigated a crime, by police, someone present moves forward to stop it, but withdraws out of fear from Meme Forces.

In May of 2014, I attended a conference sponsored by the Kingdom of the Netherlands. Their Minister of Justice announced that his country had nearly perfected a new justice system that rids itself of inner-meme (inter-departmental) conflicts. All the normally separate departments have been combined into one: police, security, arrests, indictments and JUDGES; yes judges. The result is nearly a 100% conviction rate and swift "justice;" at huge financial savings.

My thoughts, walking back to the subway were: "That's great: they arrest on Monday, convict on Tuesday, sentence on Wednesday and execute (they don't execute) on Thursday." Burials are in a different department, so they would come three days later. Here's another universal fact concerning Memes:

FIFTY-FOUR: Meme Law states: Once a person is suspected of crossing a Meme's will or violating its rules, a Meme is relentless, employing all of its members and sub-memes to neutralize the offender. Safety can be found by the suspected violator, only in a hidden sub-meme or in complete exile from the Meme's territory. Computers and electronic data systems have rendered escape nearly impossible.

Now you see why we, in the U.S., MUST get our Politicals and Enforcers UNDER CONTROL. Next, they'll come for the rest of us! It's Meme Law.

Serving as a pastor for twenty-eight years, I have lived each day with "inter" and "inner"-meme conflict. Sub-memes in conflict and Hidden Memes, trying to get support for doing what I believe we should NOT do. Talk about a short circuit! God and righteousness on one hand, church hierarchy on the other, laced all through with the need to keep my job (local church politics) and support my family.

Decision makers in all areas run into this all the time. I came across a case study some years ago where a local church needed to make a building renovation. As the Board discussed the problem in a church meeting, they determined the unit would cost $4000 and the installation would be another $2000, plus a City Building Permit for $250 dollars. The discussions produced a consensus that the church could get an outside the city contractor to install the thing cheaper and, if they did the work on Sunday the church could skip the City Permit, because no inspector would be around.

Of course, the pastor could not condone such actions and when he/she spoke up, was invited to leave the room and told to go and do "God stuff." The pastor ran further amuck by informing the board he/she would do the "God stuff" and would report their plans to the city. The pastor's argument was: "We are a church: your children are watching you, the entire town is watching you - don't you get it?" The Pastor saw the conflicting Memes here as: the church (Business Meme), its members' civic duty (Master Meme), dedication to what is morally right (God's teaching) and the Pastor's own personal need to keep a job (Family Meme). Something had to give.

FIFTY-FIVE: Meme Law states: In any "inner" or "inter" Meme conflict, some leaders involved will need to make personal sacrifices to self and personal wellbeing, even to banishment or death, if stability and wholeness is to emerge from the conflict.

A more recent conflict was found in a young family I have known for years. Here, a wife (32) was married to a husband (39); this couple found themselves as privileged members of the White upper-middle class, ex-urban, southern Meme. Republicanism surrounded everything they did (White National Meme): their neighbors, their school, their church and their friends - EVERYTHING.

During the 2012 election, which was all about getting rid of the new healthcare law (masking another "hidden" purpose to discredit our first Black President), she and I came into conflict over health care. The race question was never discussed.

Her Facebook page was wrapped in the flag replete with logos of Mitt Romney, obviously representing her deepest beliefs; which she is obviously entitled to have. The pressure on her, living where she lived, surrounded by the Republican Meme's most loyal (White Southern, well off and exurban), came not from me, but from her discovery her husband had a serious, long-term, chronic illness and they had no Health Insurance. Prior to the ACA, he was not eligible because of his pre-existing condition.

She called me to confess her fear: "This is going to ruin us." I attempted to ease her concern, reminding her that as long as Obama remains President, "in just 14 months her husband will get insurance and the family will be saved." She hung up on me and did not call for six months!

She wasn't in conflict with me; she was at war with herself, the worse type of inner-meme conflict. She was stuck - hard - between two conflicting Memes. One, her family and her husband's need for healthcare, which called her to support Obama (ACA). This was in stark contrast to her desire to fit into the Meme surrounding her, which required her support of Romney.

If she satisfied her social Meme, her husband could suffer badly for years and her family would go broke. If she saved her husband by helping elect Obama for the needed Healthcare, she was a traitor to her own neighbors. "Oh what to do?"

I don't know how she voted; I voted for her husband and family and the millions trapped without health insurance.

She will probably never realize this major American conflict had nothing to do with healthcare. Her sub-meme (tribe) is White - upper middle-class, southern suburban) this Meme felt threatened by another sub-meme, the mixed race all-American tribe (with an elected President that was Black). Just as the President of Kenya replaced the able-bodied tribes, who could handle the situation at the mall, with a more powerful Meme that could not (his tribal Meme), her tribal Meme wanted to toss out the Healthcare law to regain tribal power and retake the "White" House.

Unfortunately, this same scenario played out, even in the north. One of the world's best auto mechanics, who I have known well for 15 years, is a massive racist and a paranoid personality. His best friend found himself, also, with a serious chronic ailment. The friend begged my mechanic friend to, "Please, vote for Obama, because without the ACA "I will be through and my family destitute." At last conversation, my mechanic friend's answer was: "No matter how good he does, I just can't vote for Obama." Remember the Meme Law that reminds us that, "In Meme life there are no real friends." Never forget the two teen girls who nearly killed their friend to satisfy a fictitious Meme god.

All this may sound one-sided politically but that is not my intention. I am trying to illustrate the overwhelming power Meme membership has on us as individuals. Life and death are of little consequence to us, compared to the power of Memes over us.

One thing to understand: if you are a Police Officer, CEO, Medical Doctor or are in any positions dealing with life and death the pressure from "your people," that's your home meme (White or Black; motorcycle gang, fellow officers, insider's like you, an affiliated organization) is the one force that can grab you and make you surrender your soul and ruin your life, if you give into it.

Sadly, only one in fifty people have the courage to break their Meme's hold on them. That's why our prisons are full, suicides are legion, violence is epidemic and wars abound!

X//: MEMES, A MUST

My friend, Hank, and I were speaking of Meme activities one day. He said, after a lengthy discussion, "We just ought to rid our world of Memes, they're just no good!" After reading this book you may agree. Trouble is: we can't. I mean - we really can't.

Science tells us that each of our human bodies are covered with well over 300,000 lice and tiny mites; we are inhabited by millions of microorganisms. You can scrub forever and you won't lose them. If you could rid yourself of them, you'd die in a day. In current news stories, we are finding the antibiotics that are used in processing the animals we ingest, are entering our digestive track. These modern marvels are killing thousands of "good" bacteria, leading us to obesity and serious medical problems. Just as with the lice and the other gut livers, we are stuck together with our Memes; we need them both (Microbes and Memes).

If we were to outlaw Memes, coupling would be the first to go, no births; hospitals would disappear – no healthcare or clinics; towns and cities would vanish – no more heated homes and running water and, above all, civilization would end – anarchy would reign and life would not be tolerable.

In a few pages, we shall examine a new phenomenon, the shrinking of our social Memes. This downsizing of companies, churches and populations has created smaller Memes that are proliferating wildly and causing much social unrest.

Everything worthwhile, that we can accomplish as humans requires human minds to interconnect, exchange, share and once envisioned, work together in a Human Social Organism (family, municipality, company or country) - that's what Memes allow us to do.

The problem we still face is the one I first put forth back in chapter one – "INDIVIDUAL Human Beings are mostly good – Humankind (Memes) are equally harmful." Humankind is people gathered together in a common identity (Memes), in order to accomplish a common purpose, which may or may not reflect the good of the group or its individual members personal interests. In the end we seem to be stuck in a catch 22: Memes allow us to create Gods, Build Cities and Form Nations, BUT, Memes enable us to Unleash Devils, Make War and Kill ourselves Dead.

The very fact that Meme Law supersedes our individual consciences, where righteous behaviors are developed all through our lives, explains the harm Memes can do in spite of society's calls for righteous actions. Memes, themselves, are not easily subjected to moral development. Therefore, in taking over the individual's life, Memes mold a mostly morally inferior, fear filled being into a stronger force. But, at the same time, this "exponentializing" of the human capacity allows us to both achieve and destroy - do good and do bad.

For example, in October of 2013, a casual group of motorcyclists gathered (via social media) just outside New York City for a bike ride. In preparation for this event, a

Phantom Meme was created, as one cyclist after another emailed or Facebooked each other and made plans for the gathering.

Once gathered, the group soon evolved into an Informal Meme, seeing itself as "cycle power." In acting out, in a very self-centered way, which Memes promote in members, the cyclists soon began working together, obstructing traffic and causing havoc on the Westside Highway (NYC).

This gang was in no way a Formal Meme. It had no chief enforcer, team structure or constitution, no name or identity as a Human Social Organism. What it did have was a commonality (Collective Mind): youthful madness, a separatist, "better than them" attitude and powerful instruments (motorcycles). They were still an Informal Meme but no less a powerful force.

In the process of pushing people and bullying other drivers, one cyclist was run over by one of their victims, trying to escape. The "US' versus 'THEM" mentality, then grew out of their separatist identity. A united goal soon became "revenge on 'them' for our downed, Memed-in brother."

This is exactly what happens to police, military and other Enforcers in the doing of what they do. If a target fights back, the entire group becomes one being, an Informal Meme (thugs) inside a Formal Meme, say a Police Department. The sub-meme then turns lethal, as we have seen in police videos recently, from all over America. Let's not forget that the individual cops involved, as individuals, are still nice people, but Meme Law has taken over.

U.S. Secret Agents depend on this universal behavior when inciting riots that become civil wars. I'm sure U.S. operatives, seeking upheaval across the Arab Maghreb, North Africa, the Middle East, Ukraine (2010+), used this knowledge of baiting security forces to fire upon "innocent" demonstrators to accomplish their goal, which was: "to provoke an opposite and equal reaction," in this case civil disruption.

Many countries use this meme-up tactic, even sacrificing some of their uniformed officers as bait. They push their faces against demonstrators, so the mob will fight back, knowing: "For every action there is an opposite and equal reaction." When the people retaliate, the military can then declare them "insurgent terrorists" and ask for support from the big countries. After this, each side can mow the other down. The other side uses the same tactic. The rationale is to let a couple of your own go down, so the blood shows-up in the U.S. on TV; next, cash, weapons and power gushes into the perpetrator.

You'll note on your Six O'clock News, U.S. Planes are getting ever closer to the Russians. We were not flying before. Also, our Navy has ordered our ships to violate the territorial waters of China, nearer and nearer their new Islands. Good examples of one country pushing itself into a war posture.

Armed with this knowledge, I have to admit to friend Hank, that the biggest evils on our planet are the work of Memes, both Formal (churches, nations and corporate) and Informal (mobs, police thugs and gangs).

BUT, and at the same time, among the same peoples, almost every good done by the Human Species is the result of a Meme formation around a beneficial cause (cities, hospitals, universities, business enterprises, charities).

A few people, trying to help a community in a disaster, is good, but the Red Cross and Red Crescent can dwarf the efforts of a few people as a Meme organized for good. The American Red Cross also is a perfect example of a Meme, self-centering itself, and letting Politicians foul-up the works. As a result, the ARC grew and became more organized and, simultaneously, more corrupt, finding itself doing less and less good for each dollar.

The curse of Memes grows out of human greed, selfishness, fear and cowardice. Unfortunately, good and evil are human traits and both are "exponentialized" once attached to other human minds together in Memes. If one person can kill fifty people an hour, one-hundred people can easily kill off five-thousand people in the same hour.

But, if one person can save thirty people an hour, one-hundred people can rescue three-thousand people in the same hour.

If you believe, as I still do, that most people, at their core, seek to be righteous in most endeavors, then we must look at the Memeing process itself to view the change from Choir Boy to killer or from mother to mass murderer.

Both, as a Law Enforcement person (16 years) and as a Pastor (28 years), one of the things parents would say, when their child got into trouble, was: "She/he was a good child until he/she got in with this bad crowd!"

Unhappily, the bad in us all, becomes far worse when we're Memed-in. Within Memes, this multi-minded person in us, is enhanced, accelerated and even exaggerated, as we desire to be part of: [*insert any Meme's name here*] (Family, club, class, or religion). Each child has the ability to act out productively or act out harmfully. Membership in a Meme and the peer pressure involved, can weight this process toward either side, but, unfortunately, due to age specific forces (sex, place and self-promotion) the harmful side is over-represented.

"Memeing-in" offers a child the opportunity to serve the Meme and be accepted by adjusting her/himself to the requirement stated by the Meme. That was the first and eternal purpose of religion since ancient times, to be a child's first true meme experience. The tenets of the religion prescribe the child's duties toward the whole and promised safe entry into society in exchange for obedience.

The difficulty with Memes, whose membership is made-up of basically decent people, is the sensible center (politicians - clergy - military). This arena is often staffed by cowards or worse, "opportunists" surrendering to the ridiculous fringe or worse. Yet, many serve the Meme for their own reward and that of other insiders (Politicals). All of these self-servers are to the detriment of the Meme's family and the world it serves.

As we've seen in world-wide politics, some very harmful ideologues or deliberately selfish people, are allowed the control of social organisms and lead members into harm's way. This often results from fear, but more often for profits and, sometimes, just for the pleasure of manipulating people into destructive behaviors.

Here's the Formula for Human Horror: **GREED + FEAR + SELF-INDULGENCE + COWARDICE = EVIL!** (You'll note this is an almost IDENTICAL description of American's Social behavior pattern 1990+)

Unfortunately, for our species, these four are ubiquitous to the human condition and subject to "Emotional Contagion" of the first pathway [unthinking] (Goleman, Social Intelligence, P.324). The result is usually catastrophic, as one person or two, especially in leadership, exhibits an emotion which then spreads throughout the herd (populist) and results in a stampede throughout the entire Meme.

International governance is our only hope at buffering this contagion, by creating a governing body, above all the others, with no stakeholders, no home turf and no insider power keepers. Moses tried to do this four-thousand years ago (copied by the United Nations in 1946).

Upon gathering Israel, really a ragtag group of Mid-eastern outsiders, accidently joined by being released from slavery, Moses inherited chaos and anarchy. Each group (Sub-Meme - tribe) had its own agenda, resulting in several hundred-thousand people (recent figures tell of less than three-hundred), all members of Informal Memes, all out for their own betterment.

Moses went up to a mountain top and found a higher power, carved stone tablets with a law inscribed (attributed to the higher power) and offered it up as the basis for a new Social Organism (Master Meme), which all the subdominant memes (tribes) could be part.

By the time he returned, Emotional Contagion had reared its ugly head and the population had gone wild with our four deadly emotions. They were in a sexual frenzy worshiping animals and dangerously out of control.

With the failure of the world system of individual states post-World War II, world leaders strove again for a Moses style authority over the world's uncooperative, self-centered Memes (countries). The United Nations (Super Meme) was their answer. I firmly believe, even now, in spite of the U.S.'s attempts to derail it, the UN is Humankind's only hope.

The reason the UN has been so compromised over its existence, lays squarely in the lap of the United States. The birth of this Super Meme (UN) coincided with the standing down of the world's previous power structure (European Empires). BUT, it also coincided with the growth of an upstart, wishing to take the European's place as the world's Super Meme - The "Empire of the United States" had come of age.

So, now, we had two Super Memes, subject to Meme Law, in conflict with each other. The U.S. has used the UN as a sub-Meme to its strategic advantage by making sure this "new hope" was on U.S. soil, where it could be controlled. Also, the U.S. has been its major funder, always just underpaying and keeping the new child "barefoot and hungry." In the beginning, the U.S. refused to join without the dreaded five member veto power.

Even the USSR, initially, was ready to surrender that power, as were the Europeans, but not the U.S. Without the veto, we refused to join (just like the southern slave states, demanding slavery, had done at the U.S. becoming a nation during the Constitutional Convention (David O. Stewart. The Summer of 1787, The Men Who Invented the Constitution. NY: Simon & Shuster 2007).

At the 11th hour, the rest gave in and, ever since, the U.S. has used the United Nations, as its' own subdominant Meme, carrying out our wishes in disguise (David L. Bosco. Five to Rule Them All, The UN Security Council and the Making of the Modern World. NY: Oxford University Press, 2009).

At one time, a horribly naive "me" thought: "If only the entire earth would accept "God's" lordship that would be the answer." The main problem is, every Meme on earth has its own separate "god" and they all teach that their Meme has THE RIGHT god. In this, Religion (one of the three ruling centers in every Meme) has destroyed any concept of the Divine Power, each cutting the Creator into small pieces, each ruled by national or cultural organisms. Most of these religions completely support the annihilation or subjugation of every other group of Humans on earth.

By accepting a place in the Arena of Ideas and Beliefs as part of the Ruling Class, along with Military and Political members, all religions, of every people, have diminished themselves to becoming part of individual states and National Memes. This means they can no longer engage all people in the search for the universal quest for ultimate goodness, but, rather, are just an arm of a Governing Meme. Religion, as an avenue, meant to foster Human unity and discover the Creator - is closed, probably FOREVER.

The only hope for the voice of the sacred in Human Social affairs, is for ALL people to pull their religion out of war and governance, forcing them to deal with ALL individuals as equals and every God as one. The result, however, would be a mass defunding of religion and its loss as a "pop" icon. The flip side could be a mass trusting by the populace in "wholeness" and true peace.

For International unity and moral purposes, Nietzsche is correct, "God is dead," at least to us (a travesty in my opinion). So in the end, an independent, more powerful United Nations, remains our only possible hope.

The dramatic increase in the world's population and the corresponding decrease in separating distances, has made rule by 1500 tribes and 193 self-centered states impossible.

With humans soon to number eight billion, our planet is too small to attempt to isolate National Memes from one another. Given a Meme's nature to war against like kinds of Memes, with less space and overlapping needs, we'll never have a minute's peace, unless every National Meme is subordinated to this neutral Super Meme, which must work for the equal benefit of all and under a basic law that

all must obey. This may be the non-religious Ten
Commandments: "The Universal Declaration of Human

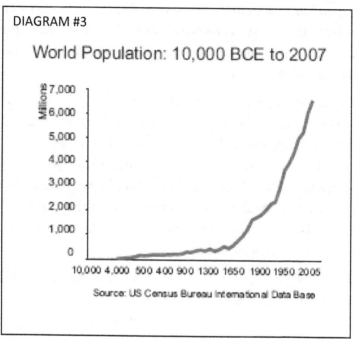

DIAGRAM #3

World Population: 10,000 BCE to 2007

Source: US Census Bureau International Data Base

Rights."

There may be just too many people on our planet to allow
separate groups, at all levels, to go unchecked, especially
now that we know how human minds and Memes work.
Now, that we understand that there are near mechanical
ways that Human Social Organisms operate. Now that
we've grown to a place where, in just two generations, we
could, easily, render the earth unable to support life; if we
can't get the very building blocks of culture - Human
Social Memes - under universal authority, we are doomed
by the power of our own brains. Remember the purpose of
Memes in society:

The social role of a Meme is to allow the Human mind to organize society by creating and operating Human Social Organisms wherein Leaders can direct; Enforcers can order; the Less connected can function and the Unconcerned can be inspired to produce. (II. Meme Basics / Meme Law)

The most negative condition in our world, is that our Memes have lost their "homeostasis"- balance. Memes, from the smallest to the largest, have always failed when one of the groups that create a Meme loses its sense of being part of that Meme. This may be, in part, due to that explosion in population numbers, causing the competition for lands, minds and economic riches to overwhelm the collective human psyche.

Whatever the reason, pure EVIL is running rampant across the globe. Everywhere: **[A]** *Alpha* LEADERS seeing their opportunity as POLITICAL rulers, disregard the others in society and "take - instead of giving" (GREED). The **[B]** *Bata* ENFORCERS take their authority and "bully it against the people - instead of and for the people" (FEAR). Our trusted **[Γ]** *Gama* CLERGY and ACADEMICS and WORKERS have misused their trusted positions in the most egocentric ways or just tuned-out (SELF-INDULGENCE). Our **[Δ]** *Delta* DROP-OUTS, have become "disenchanted, feeling or knowing, they and their work is being exploited" but are afraid of standing against power - many turn to drugs and alcohol (COWARDICE).

To this, our most fragile Group, the OUTSIDERS and MARGINALS, seeing no place or purpose, have "dropped out and party, rather than contribute." They feel: "After all, who needs people anymore?" "Shop until you drop" isn't much of a Life Goal!

Memes, in these cases, become like any other body, when any of its parts take more than it should. The result is always the same, an organism "gone bad" and an unbalanced creature that is harmful to society - That's the definition of EVIL.

Which leads me to the final, but vital point, today we deny it, but: **"There is good and evil."** We have become naturally suspicious of these terms - we are afraid of them. Religion has become so unbalanced, even the idea of right and wrong is now ignored. Forget the failure of our religions, but let us reexamine "Good and Evil" because our avoidance of them is helping with the destruction of civilization.

Sociologists, like Goleman, are forbidden the use of these terms in order to satisfy academic standards. Some will insist that one person's "evil" is another's "holy." Some claim that each of our idea of bad, is subjective, often being put forth from sick destructive Memes. Here is a test: If something is evil to one group (Meme), it cannot EVER be holy to another.

Sadly, my own country is the most guilty of this failing above all others. To the U.S., a challenger is a "terrorist," BUT when we invade another country, we have come in the name of "Democracy and Freedom." If the indigenous population fights back, they are "Insurgents" who we deem available for killing.

Because of the obvious need for change in how we humans operate our world, it appears we may now destroy civilization by our fragmented, selfish, greedy behaviors. Yet, in lieu of the disappearance of moral authority, because of the internal corruption of the same: I propose the introduction of a Preamble to Meme Law, which could be embraced by all human beings and all Human Social Organisms (humankind). If universally practiced, especially by the powerful Memes over the weaker, this may save our Human Societies and rebirth our world in peace.

The following is a suggested **"Preamble to Meme Law"**(as amended) **which states:**

(1) **Every and all Social Organisms, Master Memes, subdominant memes, lesser memes and all parties to the same, knowing how destructive our Humankind can become, shall endeavor to respect and celebrate every other Human Social Organism and all other Memes and individual persons - keeping them connected, safe and secure.** *The second part is like unto the first:*

(2) **Every Social Organism, Master Meme, Subdominant meme and all parties to the same shall care for, honor and respect all persons in their trust and all those of other cultures to the same degree that they respect themselves.**

The above may sound like a familiar religious type statement. That's because the following heroes of history have delivered nearly these same words: The Great Imam, the Buddha, Lau Tzu, Jesus Christ, Boutros Boutros-Ghali, Martin Luther King Jr., Ram Mohan Roy, Saint Paul, John Wesley, Moses, Micah, Zachariah, Charles Finney, Muhammad, James Carter and Mahatma Gandhi. These, plus thousands of Peacemakers in every land. I, Pastor Britt Minshall, am privileged to join this Meme.

I can't stress enough, **we cannot sustain our current Collective Operating Philosophy** of each interest (person or group or nation) getting all it can at the expense of others. Our competitive nature is bleeding us dead. The ultimate victim is the earth, we DEPEND on for life. As it now stands, we are hells-bent on destroying our only home and killing ourselves off in the doing of it, much sooner than ever imagined.

Even popular entertainment (movies and books) is trying to warn of our journey to self-destruction. Apocalypse literature, with us from ancient times, in the past predicted "God will do you all in." Now, the last day's literature speaks of us doing ourselves in, and it's closer than we think. Some take heart in a last minute save, such as in the 2014 movie Mockingjay: The Hunger Games Series. But, in all such cases, we are treated to a civilization in shambles - no civilization at all!

During the spring of 2014, we received two complimentary news stories that shattered even the most hardened of Social Scientists.

First, the University of Pennsylvania released results that confirmed the findings of smaller institutions: children, particularly girls, from ages six through twelve, are forming cliques (Memes) in preschool and elementary school. Further, these little ones are adept at using these mini groups to terrorize, extort and control other children in their schools.

Second, just one week later, we received a double whammy when those three, really close girlfriends, from our first page, age twelve-years, went into the woods in a Wisconsin suburb, where two ganged up on the one, stabbing her 19 times nearly killing her. This was, all to placate the "unspoken" commands of an internet cartoon "Slender Man."

So much for the unspoken agenda of seeking world peace, touted by some, predicting the ascendancy of the Female Memes over Male types. Males are seen as more combative persons. This demonstrates, as stated before: "It's not that Memes are evil, but they do allow both the good and evil inside the human being to, "exponentialize" to a much greater and far reaching degree than a solo individual could envision," Male or Female.

You see we are "stuck" with our Memes, **THEY ARE US.**

The frightening thing is, **WE ARE THEM.**

Historically, we have thought of Memeing-up or -in as an ideal situation, even though we never conceived an organized life model called a "Meme." The idea of "safety in numbers" and being accepted is embedded in us from prehistory.

I have spent the better part of twenty-years studying and facilitating groups to be effective organizations. My

"TEAM Seminars" (Together Everyone Achieves More) were well received and actually reformed stagnant Human Social Organisms (Memes) to come alive again.

Throughout this period, I believed, once the groups witnessed the good they could do working in a righteous manner, they would automatically continue in that stead. It was not so. Once I was well gone, the group gradually descended into an unproductive, many times, harmful state as before our project. That is when I began searching for, and discovered the Laws of Meme behavior.

In our current era, we are universally urbanized, connected, the entire world is ordered and we are surrounded by Mental Models (Memes) demanding our allegiance and often our lives. We all need to understand how this world system of Memes, under this Meme Law, works, lest it overcomes us and becomes us, leaving us out in the cold like castoffs. This casting off or out has become the norm over the past twenty-years.

Because of their close proximity to each other and the wild proliferation of Memes in today's world, Memes are attacking one another, rupturing and becoming smaller in size and numbers of members. This can best be seen in the reduction of employees in a certain company or industry. As pointed out earlier, many companies formerly boasting 10,000 employees (meme members) now have 800 on the rolls. Likewise, today, there may be 500 competing companies where there were formerly three. The end result is an entire generation now lives as individuals and have little or no Meme connections at all.

HEALTHY MEME STRUCTURES 1986

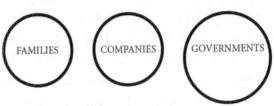

UNHEALTHY MEME STRUCTURES 2015

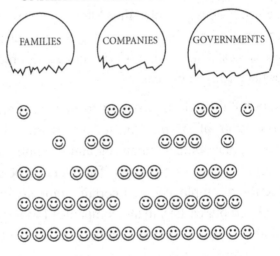

204

Often, these individuals act as informal Memes and make power plays, many beyond the pale of the law and are destructive and unaccountable.

The hope is, we become aware of the way our humanness betrays us, as well as blesses us. By being ever aware of how Meme Law operates, we'll be able to finally: Create gods (that never kill), build cities (that sustain forever) and form nations that won't unleash devils, make war and then kill us dead!

A Comprehensive Collection of
Universal Meme Laws

Memes defined: "A self-replicating cluster of ideas. Thanks to a handful of biological tricks these visions become the glue that holds together civilization (I add "any social organism"), giving each culture its distinctive shape, making some intolerant of descent and others open to diversity. They (Memes) are the tools with which we unlock the forces of nature. Our visions bestow the dream of peace, but they also turn us into killers" (Howard Bloom. NY: Atlantic Monthly Press 1995. *P 10*). **[008]**

The Purpose of Memes: The social role of a Meme is to allow the Human mind to organize society by creating and operating Human Social Organisms wherein Leaders can direct; Enforcers can order; the Less connected can function and the Unconcerned can be inspired to produce. (II. Meme Basics / Meme Law)

ONE: Meme Law states: Memes are not sticklers for truth but, being creatures of the mind (Mental Models), actually favor myths, which when adopted, by one strong Meme member can spread like wildfire to all other members, often by force, often sparking untold madness but, also, may create enormous good. [014]

TWO: Meme Law states: The social role of a Meme is to allow the Human mind to organize society by creating and operating Human Social Organisms, where LEADERS can direct; ENFORCERS can order;

the LESSER connected can function and the MARGINALS can be inspired to produce. [023]

THREE: Meme Law states: Like kinds of Memes repel and isolate from each other, similar to like poles of a magnetic force. Unlike Memes may more easily amalgamate, cluster or cooperate. [034]

FOUR: Meme Law states: Every Meme seeks to identify itself differently than others, seeing each separate identity as an establishing principle, justifying each Meme's own existence and rendering it superior to others. [037]

FIVE: Meme Law states: Individual persons have a default setting of Communion, when encountering other individuals; Memes have a default setting of Combat, when encountering other like memes. [039]

SIX: Meme Law states: The fastest, surest way to provide a Meme with identity and member loyalty is to identify an enemy threat, either internal or external, to focus member's fears and hatreds upon. [041]

SEVEN: Meme Law states: A personal relationship, no matter how well grounded, does not necessarily make a good lasting Meme relationship. [044]

EIGHT: Meme Law states: The destiny of an organism's size, structure and success is a combination of the founders' vision or the long term successor leader's vision adopted in one degree or another by the followers (cadre), which then becomes much like an organizational DNA, difficult to supplant even when the originators are all gone. [044]

NINE: Meme Law states: Memes, even international organizations, are always the most vulnerable at their base. Meme leaders should never forget in a Meme: Power comes from the center, but power's authority comes from its mass membership. [046]

TEN: Meme Law states: While Memes form the structure and platform of every Human Social Organism which gives face and structure to the Meme's concepts and principles, the Meme itself, while the real driving force of the Social Organism, remains invisible and unlocatable. [053]

ELEVEN: Meme Law states: Members at the ruling power center of a Meme, many with high celebrity status, have no power of their own and are actually prisoners of the Meme, totally subject to the Meme's will as dictated by the Power Elites and the caprice of the populace. [063]

TWELVE: Meme Law states: In the human propensity to avoid personal accountability, Memes afford the opportunity to shirk responsibility and deed that obligation to another, who will accept the rewards and the punishments. This is the route of authoritarian government and the reason people strain to avoid populace rule, seeking rather a professional ruler. [064]

THIRTEEN: Meme Law states: Once a particular group (Tribe, Family or Party) takes control of a Meme, it works to meme-in its own kind of people to operate the Meme to the exclusion of all others; thus the cadre is in solidarity in keeping control of the Meme, eventually consolidating with the position of Power Elite. [067]

FOURTEEN: Meme Law states: The most profitable method of enriching the established Meme members and keeping them safe from newcomers rebelling, is to accept small numbers of outsiders to meme-in and offer them a method for achieving insider status by accomplishing a series of unpopular and dangerous tasks. [06]

FIFTEEN: Meme Law states: Competition, as a method of expanding productivity among workers and selecting candidates for Meme leadership, even though fostering interpersonal disputes as the populace battle each other for supremacy, does create wealth which unfortunately, is almost completely driven to the center of the organism, for the benefit of Rulers and Power Elites who foster competition and combat in their continuing quest for wealth acquisition. [083]

SIXTEEN: Meme Law states: Newcomers to Meme membership are both applauded and exploited by Meme leaders, while the Meme's individual members resent the new arrivals, none-the-less, they take advantage of their newness as well. [086]

SEVENTEEN: Meme Law states: Memes always favor the acceptance of and provide for their established members and their offspring (Marginals), while they discriminate completely against Outsiders and their offspring. [088]

EIGHTEEN: Meme Law states: Meme members are inordinately loyal to their Meme. Once they are Memed-in or up they tend not to leave from external pressures, but only from internal forces and will defend their Meme to the death, even if they know their Memes position is incorrect. [092]

NINETEEN: Meme Law states: Rulers often pit one Meme member or sub-meme against another, with no rules of fairness or sense of right or wrong; the goal being the ruler's receiving enhanced loyalty from the winners and enrichment from the defeated one's losses. When invoked by the rulers, this process trumps all personal and family loyalties. [094]

TWENTY: Meme Law states: Meme members can never achieve high enough leadership, even the ultimate office, to successfully challenge the Meme's Operating Philosophy as sanctioned by the power center, without suffering consequences from others in the Meme's leadership and severe reprisals from the Meme's members. [098]

TWENTY-ONE: Meme Law states: No matter how widespread the violence of the parties in contention in an inner-meme conflict, it is always either focused on or sponsored by those in the center of the Meme in the Arena of Ideas and Beliefs, with the outer Meme members suffering the greatest consequences. Even the most populist centered movements usually have Power Elite sponsors. [103]

TWENTY-TWO: Meme Law states: The stated purpose or label given a Meme, may, often, mask another purpose entirely. [106]

TWENTY-THREE: Meme Law states: Regardless of the degree of "inner" Meme disputes, in the end the Meme must achieve Homeostasis (Balance) in order to continue to exist, otherwise it will rupture, splinter or disintegrate. [106]

TWENTY-FOUR: Meme Law states: The more Platforms (types) a Meme can claim, the more diverse its support and the greater power it can wield. Conversely, the more Platforms involved, the greater the possibility of long term unresolvable conflict. [111]

TWENTY-FIVE: Meme Law states: External pressure from other like kinds of Memes, elicits a combative defensive response from the targeted Meme, which usually requires a punitive response from the correcting Memes to achieve changes in the target Meme's behavior. This principle of other Meme interference, if pushed to the extreme, is the primary lead-up to war. [113]

TWENTY-SIX: Meme Law states: Closed Memes, more often "Belief - Blood and Beulah" located, seek to restrict membership, which often brings an end to the Meme through attrition. Open Memes, most often "Badness - Business and Boldness located," depend upon large numbers of people to achieve their goal, so these willingly expand membership accordingly. [115]

TWENTY-SEVEN: Meme Law states: When a subordinate-meme forms inside a Master Meme, it must be quietly expelled or accommodated, if not great harm or dissolution will be experienced inside the Master Meme. [117]

TWENTY-EIGHT: Meme Law states: Memes desiring to merge with other Memes, they would normally repel or conquer, in order to survive and thrive, require strong internal leadership to overcome the will of individual members, who normally reject such transplanting of Meme loyalties. This rejection is entirely visceral, caused by organizational DNA, just as our physical bodies reject transplanted organs. [118]

TWENTY-NINE: Meme Law states: Memes may have a tendency to support a gender identity, i.e., MALE or FEMALE, usually determined by the operations of the Meme being gender specific. [120]

THIRTY: Meme Law states: Meme are just as subject to universal scientific principles and physical laws as the rest of the universe. [120]

THIRTY-ONE: Meme Law states: Memes, seeking to disrupt the world at peace will work to accentuate the Meme markers of two opposing Memes (race, language, religion), resulting in a Xenophobic backlash and a "Dog Fight" style of spontaneous combative relationship. [125]

THIRTY-TWO: Meme Law states: ALL Memes are bipolar and subject to being ignited by certain triggers, the most usual of which are fear (paranoia), greed and self-interest, any, or all, of which can trigger schizophrenia (internal opposition) and render a Meme unstable and dangerous. [126]

THIRTY-THREE: Meme Law states: The most effective way to extend control over another Meme is to allow Meme Laws to divide its population into its subdominant parts, then set each at odds with the others and conquer the target Meme using, its own polar opposites to effect its downfall. [129]

THIRTY-FOUR: Meme Law states: The more powerful a Meme member becomes, the greater the opportunity and tendency to retain Meme wealth that passes his/her way for personal use. This is a consequence of a leader's requirement to completely surrender to the Meme, therefore, there is a tendency to view the organism's wealth as their personal cache'. [132]

THIRTY-FIVE: Meme Law states: The "Arena of Ideas and Beliefs" (Ruling Class) is represented in each society by the three major groups needed to control any organism. In America, and most modern states, the POLITICIANS make the rules, the CLERGY assuage the masses, and assure them the Deity has sanctioned the Meme's authority and the MILITARY (including Police) force dissenters into compliance. [132]

THIRTY-SIX: Meme Law states: In order to carry-out any act of high destruction and violence, such as war, the Arena of Ideas and Beliefs must be in total accord - The Political - The Military and The Clergy in complete agreement. [141]

THIRTY-SEVEN: Meme Law states: When a person "memes-up" or "in" to a Human Social Organism, they lose their sense of self, safety and faith in empirical data and become a different, often unrecognizable person, depending on the degree to which they surrender to the Meme. [143]

THIRTY-EIGHT: Meme Law states: Sacrifices and unpleasant tasks needed by a Meme are assigned to the newcomers and the young members, even to risking their lives; while safe and comfortable duties are carried-out by older, more established members. [145]

THIRTY-NINE: Meme Law states: Formal Memes are forever. Their structures and outward identifiers (Social Organisms) may disappear, but their force field lies in a phantom state, continuing dormant, awaiting a group with like minds and needs to reinvigorate and rebirth the dormant organism, usually with a new name. [150]

FORTY: Meme Law states: Memes are capricious and opportunistic. A Meme will sell-out its faithful, break its contracts and perpetrate mass fraud in order to protect and enrich itself and its members in Power. [151]

FORTY-ONE: Meme Law states: As the populace ignores or cowards-out of its responsibility to the whole of humankind, Celebrities or Prophets, who are powerless, will be generated by the organism to engage the people into the world from which they hide. Rarely, some become leaders, most will be discarded, but, hopefully, some of their corrective efforts survive. [154]

FORTY-TWO: Meme Law states: Memes are amoral. A Meme knows nothing of right or wrong, it only knows survival and victory over other like Memes and control of its environment. It does whatever it needs to in order to achieve its purpose and that purpose is not seen as good or bad, but "achieved" or "failed" - win or lose. [154]

FORTY-THREE: Meme Law states: Memes have short memories of member's contributions. Once a Meme member retires or is removed from participation, they will soon be forgotten. [155]

FORTY-FOUR: Meme Law states: A Meme is a here and now, an all-usurping organization that will abandon any and all agreements and solidarity with its members for the benefit of the Meme itself. [156]

FORTY-FIVE: Meme Law states: Within any Meme the greatest accolades are reserved for those at the Meme's center past and present, usually ignoring those at the outer levels of Meme life. [158]

FORTY-SIX: Meme Law states: Memes are insanely jealous and, while having little regard for their members' welfare, Memes demand every measure of their members' being. [158]

FORTY-SEVEN: Meme Law states: More powerful Meme members always abandon one of their own in times of trouble, especially one of a lower rank. Lower level members, conversely, tend to blindly support one of their own in trouble, except if the leaders order that person abandoned. [161]

FORTY-EIGHT: Meme Law states: Meme members given authority to use force on others, will do so exponentially and with little reserve. Having received approval from the Ruling Class, the target could be a close friend or family member, but, in this case, they are just victims. [163]

FORTY-NINE: Meme Law states: No one in any Meme, including churches, clubs, military and corporations - in ALL Memes, at all levels, is a true friend to any other member. The Meme authority reserves the right to encourage or disallow relations between its members, most of whom will obey the order. [164]

FIFTY: Meme Law states: The inner workings, failures and disputes within a Meme are seen as "our dirty laundry" and internal secrets, never to be discussed with those outside the Meme. [164]

FIFTY-ONE: Meme Law states: Meme leaders tend to elevate themselves and their decisions, thinking them to be sacrosanct and above other Meme members' understanding, which, in turn, adds to their sense of elitism and superiority. As a result, leaders make secret their actions, leading to social rupture, illegal actions and, often, unnecessary, internal violence. [167]

FIFTY-TWO: Meme Law states: Within a Master Meme multi-subordinate Memes will generate, some to enhance and support the work of the host's leadership; some to its detriment and even its destruction. [173]

FIFTY-THREE: Meme Law states: Memes, even if part of the same Master Meme, becoming subdominant, distrust other like Memes, even those sharing the same master and will close down or sabotage each other, if they feel threatened, rather than share for the good of all. [177]

FIFTY-FOUR: Meme Law states: Once a person is suspected of crossing a Meme's will or violating its rules, a Meme is relentless, employing all of its members and sub-memes to neutralize the offender. Safety can be found by the suspected violator, only in a hidden sub-meme or in complete exile from the Meme's territory. Computers and electronic data systems have rendered escape nearly impossible. [181]

FIFTY-FIVE: Meme Law states: In any "inner" or "inter" Meme conflict, some leaders involved will need to make personal sacrifices to self and personal wellbeing, even to banishment or death, if stability and wholeness is to emerge from the conflict. [183]

The following is a suggested "**Preamble to Meme Law**"(as amended) **which states:**

(1) **Every and all Social Organisms, Master Memes, subdominant memes, lesser Memes and all parties to the same, knowing how destructive our Humankind can become, shall endeavor to respect and celebrate every other Human Social Organism and all other Memes and individual persons - keeping them connected, safe and secure.**
The second part is like unto the first:

(2) Every Social Organism, Master Meme, Subdominant meme and all parties to the same shall care for, honor and respect all persons in their trust and all those of other cultures to the same degree that they respect themselves. [189]

Formula for Perfect Human Horror:

GREED + FEAR + SELF-INDULGENCE + COWARDICE = EVIL! [175]

Bibliography

Angelou, Maya. Celebrations. NY: Random House 2006.

Aristide, Jean-Bertrand. In the Parish of the Poor; Writings from Haiti. NY: Orbis Books 1997.

Baumol, William J.; Robert E. Litan; Carl J. Schramm. Good Capitalism / Bad Capitalism, and the economics of growth and power. New Haven: Yale University Press 2007.

Bloom, Howard. The Lucifer Principle; A Scientific Expedition into the Forces of History. NY: The Atlantic Press 1997.

Brooks, David. The Social Animal; the Hidden Sources of Love, Character and Achievement. NY: Random H. 2011.

Butler, Jon. Awash in a Sea of Faith. Cambridge MA: Harvard University Press 1990.

Cochran, Gregory and Henry Harpending. The 10,000 Year Explosion; How Civilization Accelerated Human Evolution. NY: Basic Books 2009.

Dawkins, Richard. The God Delusion. Boston: Houghton Mifflin Company 2006.

Dennett, Daniel. From Bacteria to Bach and Back: The evolution of Minds. NY: W.W. Norton; 426 pages, 2017

Friedman, George. The Next 100 Years; A Forecast for the 21st Century. NY: Anchor Books 2010.

Fukuyama, Francis. The Origins of Political Order From Prehuman Times to the French Revolution. NY: Farrar, Straus and Giroux 2011.

Gonzales, Laurence. Everyday Survival; Why Smart People Do Stupid Things. NY: W.W. Norton 2008.

Haidt, Jonathan. The Righteous Mind; Why Good People are Divided by Politics and Religion. NY: Random House 2013.

Hamid, Shadi. Temptations of Power: Islamists & Liberal Democracy in a New Middle East. NY: Oxford University Press 2014.

George, Henry. Progress and Poverty. NY: Cosimo Classics 2005 (First published in 1879 by E. P. Dutton George's writings are preserved by the Henry George Institute of New York.

Goleman, Daniel. Social Intelligence, The New Science of Human Relationships. NY: Bantam Books 2006

Isenberg, Nancy. White Trash: A 400-Year Untold History of Class in America. NY: Penguin Random House 2012

Klein, Naomi. The Shook Doctrine; The Rise of Disaster Capitalism. NY: Metropolitan Books 2007.

Lorenz, Konrad. On Aggression. NY: Harcourt Brace Jovanovich 1974

Lernoux Penny. <u>Cry of the People</u>. NY: Penguin 1980.

MacLean, Nancy. Democracy in Chains; The Deep History of the Radical Right's Stealth Plan for America. Pittsburg, PA: Dorrance - Publishing 2017

McLynn, Frank. <u>Marcus Aurelius; A Life</u>. Cambridge, MA: DeCapo Books 2009.

Parsons, Timothy H. <u>The Rules of Empire; Those Who Built Them, Those Who Endured Them and Why They Always Fall</u>. NY: Oxford University Press 2010.

Rothkopf, David. <u>Superclass; The Global Power Elite and the World they are making</u>. NY: Farrar, Straus and Giroux 2008.

Stewart, David O., <u>The Summer of 1787, The Men Who Invented the Constitution</u>. NY: Simon & Shuster 2007

Vedantam, Shankar. <u>The Hidden Brain; How Our Unconscious Minds Elect Presidents, Control Markets Wage Wars, and Save Our Lives</u>. NY: Spiegel & Grau 2010.

Watson, Peter. <u>Ideas, a history of thought and invention, from fire to Freud.</u> NY: Harper Perennial 2005.

Weiner, Tim. <u>Legacy of Ashes; The History of the CIA.</u> NY: Doubleday 2007.

Wilson, E. O. <u>The Social Conquest of Earth</u>. NY: Liveright Publishing Corp. /WW Norton, 2012.